DEDICATION

To my beloved family who have inadvertently provided so much content which made this work a labor of love.

TABLE OF CONTENTS

ACKNOWLEDGEMENTS

The author is particularly grateful for the editing efforts of Edith Leet. Her competence, corrections and suggestions are deeply appreciated. Also, Jill Preston Kross has been most helpful with her enthusiasm and in getting the book published. David Chung, from the Bay Area in San Francisco has also been most helpful in getting the manuscript published. Thanks is also due to those many individuals, particularly family and teaching colleagues, who have inadvertently provided the contents of the book.

.

INTRODUCTION

My life span which encompasses the Great Depression of the 1930s through the early years of the 2000s has to have been the most exciting in history.

In the 1930s, so many Americans had so little. With the loss of my father when I was just an infant, my mother and her brood of seven certainly lived a Spartan life. There was little money, and home keeping was extremely rigorous for a woman who, at the time, had no electrical appliances to make her tasks easier. As a family, growing up in the country, work was constant — and for us play had to be self-created. But we made it. Our family was very fortunate to have had a generous bachelor uncle and a loving, but strict, maiden aunt to pitch in with our upbringing. And, since we shifted residences between the country homestead in the summertime and weekends, to city dwelling when going to school, we had the best of both worlds.

Then came the 40s which are mostly remembered for the deprivations brought upon us by World War II, particularly the absence of my teen-age brothers who were involved in the military. Rationing of gasoline, sugar, coffee, shoes and other staples required adjustments. But the era also had the thrilling aspects of patriotism – the camaraderie of wartime mothers, the war songs, and even down to the small details including the window flags signifying someone(s) were serving their country.

For our family, post-war adjustments were fast paced. Brothers returned from the service and joined the civilian work force. The homestead experienced its introduction to electricity with the accompanying benefits of lighting and electrical appliances. Things changed at the homestead when my two older brothers bought out cousins who were no longer interested in owning the property. There then ensued a flurry of improvements by the older family members – running water, wiring throughout the house, structural improvements, etc.

The 50s ushered me into adulthood, that stage of my life where I actually enjoyed mowing lawns, good academic grades and the setting of personal goals. Even a stint in the Navy was a profitable adventure in terms of maturity — getting away from home, making friends from around the country, traveling and reveling. There then followed that euphoric stage of finding someone beloved enough to marry and start a family.

Perhaps the most exciting years were the 60s – The Civil Rights movement and the Women's Equality issues required completely revised adjustments in social action and attitudes.

That's when I started my teaching position in the local community college. Two year colleges had existed in New York State in the early decades of the 20th century, but they were either private institutions, or agriculturally-related state colleges. In the 60s all hell broke loose in terms of community college expansion. The low cost local institutions which had gotten a foothold in California, spread to New York State where some forty of them were begun with in a period of twenty years.

In theory, a student could live at home and get a thorough technical education at comparatively low cost because the financing of the colleges was a joint contribution by the state, the county of the student's residence and the student's (or his/her) family.

The expression "in theory" is used because there were unexpected developments along the way. Students weren't just local — many came from far out of the local area, including many from out of state and even from other continents. Technical emphasis was broadened by the desire of many to transfer to four-year colleges and so the more transferrable liberal arts programs thrived. Then, too, depending on economic conditions, the financing formula seemed in a constant state of flux.

Teaching and part time administration (department chair) seemed to me to be the best of both worlds. I could spend time teaching in the classroom — doing what colleges should do — and I could also do advisement and get a broader understanding of the administrative side. In that dual role, I got to know and appreciate not only my students, but administration, support staff and teaching colleagues as well. It was a great job.

The 60s was the decade of tumult. The Viet Nam War divided the nation. Authority was questioned as never before. Drugs, which had always been back there in the shadows lurking somewhere, burst forth as a unique style of enjoyment. They also destroyed many lives, including the user, his family and friends. Having late teens and early twenty year olds in class was just fun. You could cover the subject matter and at the same time enjoy the company of budding adults. Many classes were sprinkled with students in their 30s, 40's and 50's who were more serious about their academic progress, but were usually accepted by their younger classmates.

The change of pace — teaching for a most enjoyable year at the Royal Institute of Technology (RMIT) in Melbourne, Australia was a terrific experience.

The 70's ushered in the beginning of wide spread use of the computer, a technological development that changed the world. I had the advantage of starting out teaching BASIC, an easy-to-learn computer programming language. After that the pace increased sharply. Program language teaching was replaced by pre-developed software packages with an endless variety of user applications. This was quite challenging to the classroom computer teacher who was continuously experiencing change in hardware as well as software. For the accounting teacher, the influence of the computer was undeniable – however, in spite of the technology the students had to know the basic accounting principles to ensure that the software was doing its job.

In the 60's and 70's the influence of unions in education became pervasive. At first, in collective bargaining, the administration "gave away the store" (eg. granting overly-generous salary increases) but gradually it resumed command by the time the 80s arrived.

Things settled down considerably once the 80s arrived. Teaching jobs were not as plentiful — promotions were rarer and salary raises were stabilized. It was time to enjoy the less frantic pace.

My off campus life remained challenging. A brood of seven children enlivened the household. Dealing with teenagers was exhausting. There never was much money in the family, so there were fewer amenities – reliable transportation, vacations, upscale living accommodations were not for us. The children matured. Two joined the military and three attended college. There continued to be a lot of family love.

By the 90's, most of the offspring had flown the nest and my wife and I could devote ourselves to more travel, more dining out, better automobiles – and grandchildren – fifteen in all.

The first decade of the 21st century was when the decision was made to retire and to enjoy, while in good health and in modest financial circumstances, travel and leisure.

Now, in the 2010s, life is quieter; although changes continue —The Gay Rights movement has meant further attitude adjustments.

My life partner is gone, but there remains an ever-present thoughtful family to help me adjust to the golden years. As previously stated, I feel I have been extremely blessed to have lived in this great era.

W. L. Staats

Harvard on the Hudson

CHAPTER ONE—THE RETIREMENT PARTY

Off and Running

My name is Bill Stevens. I taught at Hudson College for more than forty years.

Suddenly I am on my feet to accept the award from my teaching colleagues. The occasion is my retirement bash culminating thirty-five years of full time teaching at the community college – after that I taught part time for another nine years. The award: a pedestal-mounted statuette of a horse's butt bearing the inscription: "THIS IS REALLY A FUNNY PLACE TO WORK," a favorite quote of mine over the years.

"Thanks for your thoughtful gifts, guys! First the Metamucil and then the All Bran for my bowels. Next a box of Depends, bedroom slippers that light up in the dark, clip-on gloves, and a video of 'Ace Ventura' for my very own. And now this: a statue of a horse's ass.

"How appropriate! I love it! It's me!"

The presentation of the gilded horse's butt came during an out-of-control evening that got its send-off the moment the emcee, Professor Joan Browne, took the mike. Joan, a short, salt-and-pepper-haired, feisty lady with square-rimmed glasses, a bullhorn voice, and an infectious sense of humor, had already retired and would soon once again fly off to her winter residence in Florida. She began with a monologue about the golden oldies of Boca Raton: the ladies with apricot-tinted hair who turn on their auto directional signals when they shouldn't and leave them off when they should be on.

"And you should see the elderly gentlemen spiffed up in their polo shirts, cranberry polyester trousers, white belts, and sneakers," she said. "The pants are pulled up to the chest, and the belt is cinched above the protruding gut." She demonstrated, tugging her own pants far above her waist. "Most of these guys haven't seen their private parts in years without looking in a mirror," she continued. "The Lord only knows how they manage a zipper!"

What a crowd pleaser! The guests now had an insight into the evening ahead, which for some attendants resulted in sides aching from too much laughter.

Harvard on the Hudson

Colleague Barb Houghton, a dental hygiene professor who'd started teaching at the newly constructed campus a year ahead of me, was the next speaker. She and I had been friends for three decades. Barb recalled the early years, citing archaic college policies printed in the early student handbooks, such as dress codes forbidding facial hair and sneakers, shoulder-length hair, etc. She continued with recollections of the long-since-abandoned requirement of faculty to sign in and sign out when entering and exiting the campus and of those many years of teaching at the lowest pay scale in the state. I thoroughly enjoyed her reminiscences.

"Well, I'm glad that's over!" Joan Browne groaned, back in charge of the mike. "That was the most boring bunch of garbage I've ever had to sit through." Following that outrageous insult, there was an awkward silence until Barb Houghton broke into fits of laughter. The two ladies had long been fast friends, and Barb knew exactly what to expect from Joan. It took the rest of us a moment to recognize what a great sport she was before we, too, joined in the mirth.

Next to take over the mike were a twosome of department-chair colleagues, Dolan and Andre, who had taken it upon themselves to finish cleaning out my notoriously cluttered office after my departure. "We found these in your bottom desk drawer," Dolan said, holding aloft a woman's undergarments. "I'm sure everyone in this room would love to know where these came from."

I rose to the occasion. "That's not very nice of you, guys. You must have taken those from Bob McAffrey's desk drawer. You know he loves to wear alternate gender garb on Thursday nights." MacAffrey, the arch-conservative economics professor best known for his vehement tirades against the flood of moral degeneracy inundating the world, slapped his knee and guffawed in appreciation of my gibe.

The Kissing Balls

Joan was again at the mike. "I've got to tell you a story about something that has nothing at all to do with Bill here, which surely will make it that much more enjoyable. Last week I was driving along Central Avenue, not paying attention to anything in particular, when I saw this sign outside a Christmas tree lot. KISSING BALLS, it read. That caught my attention, I can assure you. Well, I did a Uey and drove back to the lot." The guests at the retirement party were already anticipating where this monologue was leading.

"Let's talk about the KISSING BALLS," I said to the clerk. "I want to know specifically WHO does the kissing."

"YOU do the kissing. Or one of your friends," the clerk replied. "Whatever."

"I do the kissing? Why can't YOU do the kissing?"

"Whatever."

"Where do you hang these balls?"

"Over a doorway. Wherever."

"Now let me make sure I have this straight," I persisted. "I buy these balls. I take them home and hang them over a doorway. From then on, it's just a matter of people being kissed under the balls. Do I have this right?"

"Whatever."

"Well I'll be damned. That's a new one on me." Joan concluded. "I bought the balls in case anyone's interested. They're hanging in my kitchen archway. C'mon over." The attendees roared.

Room 28

I was particularly pleased when the next speaker was introduced. It was Sam Sherman, an accounting professor who had traveled in for the occasion from another college. For many, many years, he and I had enjoyed attending the annual conference of the Business Two-year College Faculty, a statewide organization of faculty and chairpersons devoted to enhancing the transfer opportunities for their students. Over the years, they'd achieved success beyond imagination at regional, state, and even national levels.

They were also a group of energetic, fun-loving individuals who brought remarkable vitality to the annual get together.

"You should all know that my main connection with Bill is on the conference circuit," Sam began. "I want to share one conference story that involves Bill, here. I'll call it Room 28—Room 28 of the Cazenovia Motel. If you don't mind, I'll paraphrase Bill and tell you the story, just as I have often heard him tell it himself."

> *The conference was at SUNY Morrisville, a small college in the center of the state. I arrived at the campus for the morning session and stayed there through lunch and then the afternoon presentations. After the conference ended for the day, I searched out the cheapest accommodations in town: The Cazenovia Motel — $32 a night — my kind of place.*
>
> *At the motel office, I was greeted by a frail, snowy-haired septuagenarian with a cigarette dangling from her lower lip. As she checked me in, we developed rapport by chatting about the fall weather and about the college where the conference was held. I had put out my cigar before*

entering the office, so I thought I'd kid her about smoking a cigarette in violation of the NO SMOKING sign over the desk.

"Are you allowed to smoke in here," I goaded.

"You bet your ass I am," she snapped back. "That sign is the owner's idea, and I don't give a shit whether he wants me to smoke or not." She winked. "I'm the manager and I do as I please. I live with my son, Wilbur, in the back. Here's your key. Room 28. Just walk down that way, open the door, and make yourself comfortable."

"Great lady. Sprightly. Lots of fun," I judged, walking toward the unit.

The room was small and neat. I unpacked my travel case and transferred the shirts, socks, and underwear to the bureau drawers. The more formal clothing went into the closet. My valise, containing the notes for a speech I was scheduled to make at the closing session in the morning, was nudged under the bed. No need to take it with me to the dinner that evening. Next I paid a visit to the john. Not bad, I thought, noticing the paper strip wrapped around the toilet seat. I broke the strip before using the facility and then indulged myself with a refreshing shower. Then I left the unit to go to dinner.

Traditionally, the annual conference dinner was held at one of the host college's better local eateries. It was invariably a congenial gathering featuring great conversation, fine food, and an abundance of liquid refreshments. Table-hopping to briefly visit with colleagues from other campuses across the state was customary. The festivities lasted well into the evening, culminating in story and joke telling over stimulating snifters of brandy. What a great evening we all had!

It must have been near midnight when we went our respective ways. Cautiously, I drove back to the Cazenovia Motel, parking in front of unit #28. I studied the key with sodden deliberation before trying it in the door. Right key, right door. I was looking forward to a good night's sleep.

What a shock awaited me as I entered the room. I couldn't believe my eyes! None of my possessions were there. No clothes in the closet, nothing in the bureau drawers, no valise under the bed! There was also a bizarre situation in the john — the paper wrapper was once again neatly sealing the toilet seat! Panic set in. Again and again I checked the room number and the key.

"Everything's gone!" I yelled into the night. "I've been set upon by thieves."

Harvard on the Hudson

I stumbled to the motel office, banging on the door after reading the CLOSED FOR THE NIGHT sign. No response. More banging. Finally a light. The septuagenarian groggily opened the door. "What a metamorphosis," I thought to myself, seeing this same little old lady in hair curlers, wrapped in a well-worn robe. She didn't seem quite as sprightly as the person I'd met earlier.

"What's wrong?" she asked groggily.

"Wrong! Everything's wrong. When I got back to my unit, all of my clothes were missing. Everything else is too, including my valise full of notes that I've got to have in the morning. Someone has stripped my belongings from my room!"

"Oh my," she responded. "Wait right there while I wake up my son." She disappeared into the back room, and I could hear her calling, "Wilbur! Wilbur! Wake up! There's a problem! Wake up, Wilbur!"

Eventually Wilber shuffled into the motel office. He was a fiftyish hulking dollop, unshaved and unkempt, clad in baggy pajamas and wearing scuffed-up slippers. He was tired, and he wasn't happy.

"What's going on?" he mumbled.

"None of my belongings are where I left them in my room!" I cried. "I'm lost without my valise, and I

just don't know what the hell has happened! I think the room has been broken into. But there is one peculiar thing—the wrapper is back on the toilet seat. I distinctly remember removing it."

Wilbur picked up a flashlight, and we proceeded to Room #28. He stealthily opened the door. What a thorough search ensued. Every bureau drawer was opened and closed and reopened. The bedding was pulled down. He even got down on his hands and knees and then on his sizeable gut to look under the bed. After confirming the situation for himself, he made a most unsettling comment. "Must be those damned Graber boys down the road. They've broken in before. I wouldn't put it past them. Damn those kids!"

"But why would they put the wrapper back on the toilet seat?" I asked. Wilbur pondered the question. "Maybe the cleaning lady came around. But she only comes by in the morning." Wilbur was as confused as I was. "Let's go back to the office," he suggested.

As we closed the door behind us on Room #28, Wilbur gave a startled look at the adjoining unit. "Wait a minute. There's a light on at unit #29. We didn't rent that out today. Let me see what's going on." He knocked on the door. No response. He knocked again. Still no response. With that, he took out his master key and unlocked the door to #29.

I followed him inside.

Low and behold, it was all there: my luggage, the clothes in the closet, the valise under the bed, and the socks and underclothing in the bureau. Furthermore, the toilet seat was stripped of its wrapper!

The mystery was solved!

Apparently my key to Room #28 fit others of the motel unit doors as well. I'd used it earlier in the day to get into #29 without looking carefully at the room number, and the damned key had worked.

What a feeling of relief swept over me. While I apologized to Wilbur for disturbing his sleep, I couldn't help but wonder why my key fit other rooms.

Sam and I were scheduled to meet for breakfast the next morning. In a nearby donut shop, over coffee and juice, I spilled out the details involving Room 28. Sam absorbed it all, shaking his head from side to side. "My friend," he gravely said when my story was completed, "I want you to do both of us a favor. When we get to the conference, don't, whatever you do, don't tell this story to the others. It's beyond embarrassing."

At this point, I asked Sam for the microphone. "How about letting me finish this," I said." I'm afraid you might be inclined to leave out the rest of the story." Sam handed me the mike.

"What a thoughtful guy," I said to myself. "He's trying to prevent me from embarrassing myself."

After breakfast Sam drove off to the conference. I returned to Room #29, packed up my belongings, and give back the multi-purpose key to the attendant. After apologizing profusely to the lady for my somewhat berserk behavior, I left and went to the SUNY Morrisville campus.

The morning sessions are always preceded by a warm-up offering of coffee, juice, and Danish pastries.

As I entered the doorway, everyone stopped what they were doing and stared in my direction, then broke into gales of mirth. "There he is—the survivor of the Room #28 break in!" someone announced. Jeers and cheers followed.

So much for Sam's confidentiality!

When Sam started this story I thought to myself that it was a "you'd have to have been there" story, but the enthusiastic applause following the concluding remarks indicated otherwise.

Harvard on the Hudson

The Family Pitches In

My son, Grant, had been selected by his six siblings to speak on behalf of the Stevens family. In his mid-thirties, Grant had grown up to be a handsome, physically fit, good-natured, and considerate young man with a keen sense of humor and a very likeable personality. He was an officer in the Naval Reserve and justifiably proud of his accomplishments as a Navy SEAL.

"Growing up in my house was like spending my early years at the Norman Bates Motel," Grant began, making reference to Alfred Hitchcock's movie "Psycho."

"Here we go," I thought to myself. "The others *would* choose *him* to carry out the family testimonial assignment. This will be full of half-truths, non-truths—anything to milk the crowd for laughs."

Grant already had them in the palm of his hand by using the Bates Hotel reference. "My Dad is quite a guy, as I'm sure you are all aware. But I want to tell you some things you may not know."

I swallowed.

"Dad broke my brother Greg's leg when he was only three years old. Today we'd call that child abuse." He paused.

"Just a minute!" I interrupted, rising to my feet. "It was an accident. I was watering the lawn with a garden hose, and I gave it a good yank to get more length. How was I to know the damned kid was standing in the coiled part of the hose behind a big bush where I couldn't see him?"

"He practically cut off my sister's finger with a kitchen knife," Grant continued. She was only two years old at the time and still has the scar to prove it!"

"There's more to that story," I broke in defensively. "My wife, Sandy, was working, and I was left in charge of the kids. I was making tuna sandwiches for my young family who were sitting around the table. Just as I was cutting a sandwich in half, the two-year old slipped her forefinger under the bread as I cut down. At the time I had become distracted by a beautiful red cardinal that had perched outside of the window. Not thinking about the knife, I bore down pretty hard, surmising that there was a bone in the tuna fish. Good thing she let out a yelp."

"He left my sister Giss in the supermarket—sitting in the grocery cart! They had to call Mom to come and get her."

"Excuse me, please," I interjected. "Sandy had sent me shopping with a list of groceries that filled up three carts. For heaven's sake, give me a break! I remembered the groceries, didn't I?"

Showing no mercy, Grant continued, "And then when Giss was only two, Dad lost track of her, and she sank to the bottom of the river."

"Point of order!" I wailed. "I had Giss standing on the ladder down at the swimming area. I wasn't doing too bad a job of keeping track of her until this beautiful yacht sailed by. Talk about being distracted! When I turned back to see how Giss was doing, she had disappeared. There was only one place she could have gone—to the bottom of the river. About 8 feet down! I swam down and sure as hell, there she was—holding her breath and sort of waiting for me at the foot of the ladder. Cutest thing you ever saw!"

"When we were old enough to swim a distance, Dad used to herd us into the river, goading us to swim across the quarter-mile stretch. One time we were nearly chopped up by the huge vegamaster propeller of an ocean-going tanker churning its way down river."

"Guilty as charged," I admitted.

The stories continued. They were all half-truths, but the siblings nodded in agreement as he proceeded through the list.

Toward the end of his talk, Grant changed his tone and became sentimental, praising me for being such a terrific father. By the time he concluded, there wasn't a dry eye among the attendees. Resounding applause followed his talk.

With rapid dispatch, Joan Browne changed the mood. "How did a homely guy like your father ever produce a handsome dude like you?" she asked Grant. "I could really use a boy toy around the house. If you're interested I'll give you my phone number, honey. We can get started anytime you're ready!"

Winding It Up

Two other teaching colleagues, Tim Hunter and Lou Rosmino, took on the more serious task of the evening — presentation of gifts. A handsome plaque, cleverly citing my fondness for cheap cigars, my pathetic piano playing, and my spontaneous laughter, had been created by Sue Strong, yet another colleague. Finally, Sandy and I were called to the microphone as the last of the gifts, an envelope containing a wad of traveler's checks, was presented. How appropriate for a couple about to embark on several global adventures.

The Dean of the School of Business, my immediate superior, was the last of the speakers. He'd put up with my shenanigans over many years and was clearly relieved at the prospect of peace and quiet following my departure from campus.

"This has to be the happiest day of my life," he said. It didn't much matter what followed. That introductory remark said it all, and it really hit the target dead center.

Following my closing comments—more in the form of a rebuttal—a DJ did a masterful job of keeping the crowd on the dance floor until the early hours of the morning.

As things wound down, I clutched the statue of the horse's butt. *THIS IS REALLY A FUNNY PLACE TO WORK* read the inscription. "How fitting," I reflected. And reflected and reflected about my thirty-eight-year teaching career.

CHAPTER TWO—PRACTICE TEACHING AND THE HIGH SCHOOL YEARS

I recalled the very beginning of my teaching career, which started with eight weeks of practice teaching in the village of Chatham, a forty-five-minute drive from home. Practice teaching is that part of the teacher education program where a budding schoolteacher is sent off campus to work with a master teacher, an experienced mentor, who undertakes a supervisory role, guiding the student teacher as he/she takes over the master teacher's classes for several weeks.

My master teacher, Justin DeLyson, couldn't have been a nicer guy. Folksy, good-natured, and casual, he and his wife had been teaching for several years in this friendly, small, country town where the high school faculty seemed to be one big family. I was lucky to get the assignment.

Harvard on the Hudson

An Auspicious Beginning

After watching Justin teach for a day or two, I was on my own. This was Justin's style: don't interfere with the practice teacher, just let him do his own thing and smooth out the rough spots in private once the class has been dismissed.

I was a nervous wreck. There was so much to keep track of: the plan book, the attendance register, the sea of young faces staring up at me, seemingly waiting for me to make a mistake. Yet I made it through the first class without a hitch. From then on things would go easier. That first class is always a killer. Justin was seated in the back of the room, monitoring my performance.

"Well, Justin, how did I do," I asked anxiously.

"Everything seemed to go pretty well," Justin said reassuringly, "but there was one slight problem you've got to take care of."

"What's that?" I asked.

"Your fly was open throughout the entire class." Justin smiled.

An auspicious beginning.

Intercom Antics

I clearly recalled other early classroom experiences, such as the time an intercom announcement sent my class into gales of laughter. Chatham was a small school with all grade levels under one roof. To communicate a message over the intercom, it was necessary to broadcast into every classroom.

I was teaching business law at the time. My classroom of juniors and seniors hushed to silence as the announcement began.

"There have been adjustments to the bus schedule because of mechanical problems," a voice rasped through the intercom. "Please take note that the children who usually take the bunny bus will be using the alligator bus."

The announcement hadn't run very long when it became obvious that the message was directed to the Kindergarten, first, and second grade classes, but I had to let it run its course.

"Those who normally go to and from school on the turtle bus will go on the turkey bus," the message continued. "The pony bus people will be riding on the tiger bus, and the rooster bus children will be using the elephant bus."

It was difficult for me to maintain order among my high school charges when I couldn't stop myself from laughing.

"For the sake of avoiding confusion, let me repeat this announcement," the voice continued. And so it did. And so the merriment in my classroom continued.

Harvard on the Hudson

A Case of Mistaken Identity

Taking attendance in each class is mandated by state law. As a law-abiding teacher, I dutifully fulfilled this responsibility. It was never easy at the outset of the school year. I didn't know one student from another, so I would read out the name and then ask the student to raise his/her hand to indicate being present, as well as to help me get a handle on who was who.

As the days passed and I got to know the students, the attendance procedure became less laborious. But in one of the beginning sessions, an awkward situation occurred.

"Patricia White," I called out, reading from the class roster. Then, assuming I could kill two birds with one stone, I read out the next name: "William White."

A thought flashed through my mind before I looked up to see whose hands were raised. Both had the same last name, and both were at the same grade level.

"Are you two twins?" I asked.

A ripple of laughter spread across the classroom. My face reddened when I saw that Patricia was African-American and William was Caucasian.

The High School Years – Full-time Teaching

The eight-week practice teaching experience assured me that I'd chosen the right profession. The following autumn, I began a four-year career as a full-time secondary school business teacher in a school with some thirty faculty and an extremely capable principal. My assignment was mostly in the area of secretarial subjects, including shorthand and typing. Computer courses were two decades in the future.

Dealing with Teen Age Girls

The shorthand class had 20 sophomore girls, and, oh, were they sometimes tough to deal with! Close-knit friendships would cement and disintegrate at whim. I strived to make the classroom more appealing by having my female charges responsible for a change of the bulletin boards each month. The students were asked to work in small groups, choosing their own team. I set up the schedule for the entire school year. The girls came up with some imaginative ideas of decorating the bulletin boards with attractive presentations relating to the importance of secretaries in business.

All went well for the bulletin board presentations in September and October. I was so proud of my charges that I invited the principal and my teaching colleagues to stop by to admire the displays.

Disaster struck in November. There was no visual presentation, just two bare bulletin boards. I wasn't happy about the negligence of the three girls who were responsible for the display.

"I'd like to meet with Jesse, Sally, and Mary after class," I announced.

It didn't take me long to realize that close friendships among high school sophomores can sometimes be a fleeting experience. I learned that Jesse was dating Mary's boy friend, and that Sally had made an unkind remark about Mary's new hairstyle, and that Mary was having nothing to do with either of the other two. None of this, of course, came to me through any of the three girls. Their chatty classmates filled in the details.

All bets were off regarding the schedule for the rest of the year. I decided to revise the assignments on a month-by-month basis, hoping that newly formed friendships would last at least that period of time.

The Car Wash

Along with my teaching duties, I was assigned the dubious honor of serving as advisor to the Junior Class. Within short order, I learned that fundraising was part of the advisor's responsibilities. Funds were needed to help finance the yearbook, athletic events, class rings, the prom—the list went on and on.

What to do to raise money? Leave it to the students themselves to come up with an idea.

"I think my dad would let us use his filling station for a car wash some Saturday," George Kospky suggested.

"Excellent," I said, endorsing the suggestion. I'd been homeroom teacher and advisor to the group for several months. Several of them were in my classes, and rapport had been swift and solid.

George later confirmed that his dad was willing. A date was set for a Saturday late in April. The students made "Car Wash Here" signs, and a dozen or so agreed to be on hand. It all seemed to be coming together.

That spring Saturday, the weather cooperated beautifully. Bright sunshine — temperatures in the low 70's — great day for a car wash. Nothing could cast a shadow over the event, right? Wrong!!

I and a few other students arrived early in the morning.

Ah, the glories of the garage! Huge calendars featuring photographs of voluptuous women in the buff adorned every wall. Remember, this was in the '50s, a more Victorian era. The guys in the junior class were agog, the girls were embarrassed, and I was horrified!

"I'll just have to keep them out of doors," I noted to myself, ushering the youngsters to their task stations. "And won't it be fun when the principal shows up? He promised to support the car wash. The rest of the faculty will relish my discomfort, too. Damn!"

Harvard on the Hudson

But the naked women weren't the worst of it. George's dad, a hard-working mechanic, had stipulated that he would be working in the grease pit and garage throughout the day. As an unending stream of cars pulled in for a clean-up, it was difficult to manage a conversation with the customers. George's dad was apparently having a bad day, and the endless succession of curse words emanating from the grease pit were loud and clear.

"You whore!" he shouted into the engine of a troubled Dodge.

"Rotten bastard," he cursed when a spring pinched his hand.

"Motherf——-'' wafted out of the grease pit—several times.

My stomach was in knots. The guy was in no mood to be talked to. The students, on the other hand, were having time of their lives: making money, playing grab ass, and thoroughly enjoying Mr. Knobsky's colorful vocabulary.

Somehow, the principal came and went, totally oblivious of the goings on. Somehow we all got through what seemed to be the longest day of my life.

Working with a Maiden Lady Supervisor

Harriet Stupples wore tailored suits. She was in her 60's—silver hair, steel-rimmed glasses, short and trim. She was not married and never had been. She was also a very strict disciplinarian. As chairperson of the Business

Department, she supervised three male faculty, including me, and I was almost as afraid of her as were her students. To make matters more complicated, Harriet and I shared the same desk in a classroom. The school simply had no extra office space.

"How can such a diminutive lady hold so much authority over the students?" I wondered. "Some are literally terrified in class. They never get out of line as they sometimes do with me." I was envious.

It didn't take long to find out Harriet's secret for maintaining discipline. She could be moody — and she could be mean-spirited — and she could even lie like hell. But it worked.

On one occasion, I was incredulous when I overheard her admonish her junior class homeroom, "You'd better behave yourselves, or I won't *vote* for you to become seniors!!"

Vote students to become seniors? That's a new one on me.

And poor Henry Melzer. She had him so unnerved that he wet his pants during the typewriting final. She had sternly taken him to task when the paper came right out of the machine and he continued typing on the roller. He was so obediently following her instructions not to look at the keyboard that he never noticed that the paper was missing. When she launched into her diatribe, his kidneys gave way and he bolted for the boy's room.

Harriet later confessed that she was afraid the kidney overflow might have electrocuted the young man who was operating the new electric IBM.

She was occasionally moody with me, too, even though we eventually came to like each other. Because we shared the same desk, I would subtly find out when I was in the doghouse.

The first time this occurred was after a department meeting with the principal, who was an excellent administrator with a keen sense of humor. Harriet was voicing a lament that had plagued business teachers for years and years: the poor quality of students counseled into the business department.

"We're tired of leftovers," Harriet said, directing her displeasure to the principal.

"Harriet, we mustn't speak of the students as though they were yesterday's baked goods," he cleverly responded. I roared with laughter. Harriet cast me a frozen glare. The next day, I couldn't find my tape dispenser. It had been on the desk but now was nowhere to be found. Since Harriet wasn't speaking to me after the department meeting incident, I couldn't ask her about it. Months later, I found it hidden in the file cabinet.

"Why that old fox," I thought, making a mental note for the future.

Eventually our frosty relations thawed. Not too much time passed, however, before I couldn't find my scissors. Then I remembered that Harriet and I had had a disagreement regarding a student's grade.

"Aha!" I exclaimed as I discovered the scissors in yet another file cabinet.

At later dates there were the incidents of the missing pen and the missing box of staples and the missing packet of rubber bands. Eventually, however, this novice teacher and the department chairman became very close friends.

There was one last rupture. It was in my fourth and final year before I took the job at the community college. The principal hosted a whopper of a Christmas party at his home. For some reason, Harriet got into the martinis—and well into the spirit of the season. For Harriett it was a Dr. Jeckyl-Mr. Hyde transformation. She told jokes, she laughed, and she even danced. At one point she located a girdle in a closet, pulled it on over her suit, and joyfully paraded among the happy crowd. Someone discovered that it would be neat to snap the elastic stocking clips attached to Harriet's girdle, and several others joined in the snapping fun

The next day was a dark one for Harriet—and for anyone within reach. She was sorely embarrassed by her own actions. I didn't help matters by assuring her that she was "at her best." That's when my ruler disappeared.

Harvard on the Hudson

The Yearbook Debacle

Teenagers can sometimes wear you down.

In addition to teaching, I had also taken on the responsibility of advisor to the high school yearbook committee. There was so much to do, and it took so much time: student photos, descriptions of the student's activities while in school, a "cutesy" poem describing each graduating student, club photos, the class gift, dedication to a favorite faculty member, the class will, projections for the future, sports photos, and on and on and on! The development of the yearbook took up a good part of the academic year.

Regardless of the thoroughness and industry with which my charges and I went about our work, panic set in toward the academic year's end. Where were the proofs? Why didn't a particular article get completed? Where were some of the committee members when they were most needed? At times my stomach was in knots. Sleep didn't come easily.

At last the work was complete. The only remaining task was to have the yearbook contents delivered to the print shop. (It should be noted here that this was long before the advent of the computer. Duplicating the production in time for graduation would have been impossible).

With enthusiasm the student committee assembled in my office. It was agreed that the most responsible ones, George, Elaine, Patty, Margo, and Mike, would put the materials in George's car and drive them to the printing office, which was located about fifteen miles from the high school. When the last of the boxes was carted out, I closed my office door. "A good job well done," I sighed with satisfaction. "I thought we'd never get to this point."

Late that evening, I received the phone call that initially sent me into panic — followed by deep, deep depression.

"Mr. Stevens," George began in a croaked whisper, "I have some very bad news about the yearbook materials. We decided to put the stuff in Mike's convertible. Mike, Elaine, and I sat in the front seat. We put the boxes of yearbook stuff in the back seat. It was such a great day that we put the top down."

"Oh, no!" I interrupted. "No, you couldn't have. But get on with it. What happened?"

"It was really windy, Mr. Stevens. We were driving along, listening to the top tunes on the radio, and singing at the top of our lungs. Never once did we look back to make sure the yearbook stuff was okay. Would you believe that we had left the boxes open and that the wind scooped just about everything out of the boxes and scattered it all along the route for about a ten-mile stretch?"

I sank slowly into my chair. "Yes, I believe that, George. I have no trouble at all believing that. Were you able to collect it all, George?"

"Only some of it, Mr. S. Lots got lost in that marshy farm area just outside of town. There was so much mud, and the cows were stepping on the stuff and everything!"

It was decided to publish the retrieved materials, resulting in the thinnest yearbook in the history of the school.

The yearbook incident was a factor in my decision to move on to teaching at a higher level of education: the community college.

CHAPTER THREE—VALHALLA—THE COMMUNITY COLLEGE

(Dubbed "Harvard on the Hudson" by some anonymous wit)

Getting the Job

The community college movement swept across New York State in the 1960s. I had four years of teaching experience at the secondary school level. Moving on to the community college seemed to be a desirable career change. It would mean working with more mature students who were paying for their education. Besides, the new college was only ten miles from home.

I interviewed for the teaching job at a dilapidated, converted shirt factory located in downtown Troy. A new campus would be up and running in the fall semester. One business teacher was being hired. I didn't get the job but was offered the position of business manager. I declined. I loved teaching and had no aspirations for administrative work. A year later, when enrollments began to swell, college president Otto V. Gunstrom telephoned me to arrange an interview. As a result of that successful experience, I was offered a full-time teaching position. In March, I gave my resignation notice to the principal at Hudson High. I would be leaving at the end of the academic year.

I started at the college in the fall of 1961. I never regretted this decision. Hudson College was truly a fulfilling place to work in so many different ways.

The Autocrat

The first president of the community college was a man in his sixties. He was a bachelor, clean but rumpled looking, with thinning hair, a paunch, and glasses. A seemingly endless stream of cigarette smoke drifted from his nose. When he talked, it was more like a series of grunts. If you were to look up the word "autocrat" in the dictionary, it's just possible there'd be a photograph of Otto V. Gunstrom to reinforce the written definition.

His philosophy for success was to hold the tightest reins possible. His management style somewhat resembled that of the nineteenth century industrial despots. His were the only final decisions. The purse strings he held tightly in his grasp. As an illustration of his tight-fisted approach to controlling costs, faculty were required to sign a receipt when procuring pencils, paper, and chalk.

The stories about Otto became legend. And they were all true.

The Toaster

George Geneva was hired on as cook and manager of the cafeteria. At the time, some 1,000 students attended the college, and it was George's job to provide breakfast for those with early classes as well as meals and snacks later in the day. His main problem was the equipment he had to work with, particularly the toaster, which made only two slices at a time. It had two doors hinged at the bottom, which held the toast up to the heating element. Once one side of the bread was toasted, George had to open the doors, turn the bread around, and close the doors until the reverse side was done. Then he took the toast out of the machine. All of this while a line of students waited to be served. It was an appliance straight out of the 1930s, a relic of a bygone day that was grossly inadequate and inefficient.

"For years I begged that man to buy me a commercial toaster," George would tell his sympathetic colleagues. "He finally gave in and had the college buy me a *used* one, with the stipulation that I would sell the antique. Do you know that that cheap bastard constantly bugged me about selling that worn out piece of shit? Finally I gave him $2 for it out of my own pocket just to shut him up!"

The Adding Machine

Ah, but Otto V. Gunstrom was cunning, and he prided himself on that. One of the young members of the engineering department faculty, Paul West, was sneaking home one of the college's adding machines to help him make calculations in his side job as a consultant.

Paul was crafty at avoiding detection. Somehow Otto got wind of Paul's little game but was unable to catch him in the act. He'd lurk behind doors in the late afternoon, but to no avail. Paul's stealth was too much for Otto to endure. The wily president knew it would be useless to confront Paul unless he had proof, so he decided to use a different tactic. He knew the adding machine was being borrowed from the secretarial pool and that the secretaries liked Paul and wouldn't deliberately turn him in.

Otto decided to confront a secretary directly.

He startled Ella Hacker in the hallway after she came out of the ladies room. Almost everyone was afraid of Otto, and he knew it.

"Ella, you've been stealing an adding machine and taking it home at night!" he thundered in a threatening tone.

Shocked and frightened, Ella gasped, "Oh, no, Mr. Gunstrom. I haven't been stealing anything. That was Paul West!" As soon as she blurted out the culprit's name she clasped her hand over her mouth. Too late—the damage was done! The old cougar had won again.

Paul was duly reprimanded.

Poor Ella

Once Otto learned that he could intimidate someone, that person became prey to his bullying techniques. Such was the case with poor Ella Hacker who had ratted on Paul West without meaning to.

At an off-campus Christmas gathering, Ella came dressed to the nines, topping off her ensemble with a fur stole she'd inherited from her aunt. Ella had little personal wealth, and her pay at the college (as well as that of all other employees) was meager to say the least. But she managed to keep herself dressed fashionably.

Harvard on the Hudson

Not long after Ella had made her entrance, Otto Gunstrom approached her with a stern look in his eye. "Ella, that's some fur stole. How can you afford it? We must be paying you too much money!"

Flustered and close to tears, Ella began to sputter about where she got the coat. Otto, refusing to listen, shook his head and disappeared into the crowd.

Fresh Air vs. Heat Loss

In the '60s, personal computers had not yet made the scene. Their forerunners were comptometers, adding machines, cumbersome banking machines, electric typewriters, and so forth. One of my teaching assignments involved a course called Office Machines offered in a well-lighted, second story corner room with banks of windows along two walls.

I liked the location. When the students were busy, I could idly gaze out the windows watching the campus traffic. Now and then, I'd spot President Gunstrom's car coming onto the campus.

One afternoon, not long after Otto came into the first floor entrance, I heard a knock on the Office Machines classroom door. When I opened the door, there stood Otto V. Gunstrom. I was as afraid of the old coot as the next person, but he maintained a cheery smile.

"Hi, Mr. Gunstrom. Gee, it's good to see you!" I lied, quaking in my shoes. "What can I do for you today?"

The president seldom minced words. "Stevens, I notice that you don't have any windows open. These students are breathing stale air and probably getting sleepy. Get some life into this place. Open some windows for God's sake!"

"But Mr. Gunstrom," I responded, ready to remind the old man that it was bitter cold outside on that February day.

Before I could get my point across, Otto exited, slamming the door behind him.

I knew when I'd received an order. The following day, I made sure the windows were wide open. The students huddled in their seats, clasping their arms around themselves to keep warm. But, damn it, they were getting healthy fresh air!

Once again there was a knock on the door. Upon opening it, I came face to face with Otto, who was glowering menacingly.

"Stevens, what's the matter with you? Close those windows! What are you trying to do — heat the county?"

This time I had no response. Again the door slammed shut.

Otto was a master of the "No win" situation.

Harvard on the Hudson

The Inquisition—You Lose, McCaffrey

Otto V. Gunstrom's complete authority was manifested in yet another way: the yearly inquisition. Each faculty member was annually subjected to a "review," which consisted of a personal interview with the college president. During these sessions, Otto was in total command because the results determined whether or not the faculty member would get another year's contract and how much of a raise, if any, it would contain.

Needless to say, with so much riding on the results of this grueling session, the interviewee was often completely unnerved lest he or she make the wrong impression.

Since the college was new, most of the faculty were very inexperienced, and few had ever dealt with the likes of Otto V. Gunstrom.

McCaffrey, newly hired as an economics professor, anxiously awaited his annual meeting with the president. The poor fellow had spent his first year trying to manage with a teaching load of eighteen hours a week involving preparations for four different courses. He was barely able to keep up, let alone get ahead, in terms of preparations.

"McCaffrey, where are your notes?" Otto demanded.

"My notes? What notes are you talking about?"

"The typewritten notes you use as a guideline during your class teaching. Surely you have typewritten notes!" Otto glowered.

"All I have time to do is handwrite an outline of what I'm going to cover in class. They're just sketches. Nothing formal. I don't have time to type them."

"Hmmph," Otto interrupted. "The next time you come in here for your interview, I expect to see your notes. Do you understand?"

Cowed, McCaffrey made his apologies and departed, assuring the president he would comply with his request the next time around. Fortunately, McCaffrey was issued another contract containing the same meager $300 raise that was offered to most of the others.

The following year, McCaffrey came to the interview prepared to the hilt. He had volumes of typewritten notes, which had cost him and his wife untold hours of work.

Proudly McCaffrey set down his compilation: four binders bulging with neatly printed material.

"What's all that stuff?" Gunstrom asked.

"My notes, Mr. Gundstrom. I've brought along all of my class notes!"

Otto glared at the display and incredulously remarked, "Is that all you have to do with your time is write notes,

McCaffrey?" "What about guest speakers, field projects, term papers?"

The professor was flabbergasted — just as Otto had planned.

When McCaffrey came away from the interview, he just shook his head back and forth in dismay.

Stevens Gets Grilled

Bob McCaffrey and I were good friends. When I learned about Bob's experience with Otto, I was terrified, since my interview was scheduled for the next day.

I, too, was barely keeping up with my preparation and teaching of five different classes, Statistics, Business Math, Office Machines, Real Estate, and Insurance. About the last two courses, Real Estate and Insurance, I was particularly unsure of myself, because I had so little personal experience with the subject matter.

Thanks to well-written textbooks, the content could be absorbed with repeated reading. With so much to digest, I was often only a few pages ahead of the students.

Otto had more than one zinger up his sleeve. Sometimes he would ask the professor a searching question about an obscure area that he'd looked up using the table of contents. Oh, he was a sly one! If the professor wasn't able to come back with a satisfactory answer to Otto's question, he knew he was in deep trouble.

Such was the case during my annual interview.

The term "re-insurance" appears in insurance textbooks. It refers to the situation whereby an extremely valuable piece of property (e.g., the Empire State Building) is worth so much that no single insurance company would dare to cover it. In such a case, the insurance risk would be shared with other insurance companies. Hence the term re-insurance.

I was somewhat familiar with re-insurance, since I had discussed it with my class.

Unknown to me, however, this was to be Otto's key to catching me off balance. Previous to the interview, Otto had gotten hold of the insurance textbook and was prepared to lay his trap.

He posed the question in a way that I simply couldn't understand what he was looking for in terms of a response. The old man asked, "Alright, Stevens, tell me this. What would you do with a large insurance policy?" He took a long draw on his cigarette.

I swallowed. I hadn't the foggiest idea what the president was talking about. Not a clue. So I said what immediately came to mind.

Timidly I responded, "What would I do with a large insurance policy? I think I'd fold it up!"

There was an awkward pause.

Fortunately the old cougar had occasional bouts with humor. With smoke billowing from his mouth and his nostrils, he broke into a hearty laugh, slapping the desk in appreciation of the unexpected response.

I sighed with relief.

The interview continued. "Stevens, why don't you dress better?" referring to my somewhat tattered vest and rumpled shirt.

I gave him an honest answer. "I can't afford better clothes yet, Mr. Gunstrom. I have six children, and I'm spending what extra money I have on advanced courses, books, and car repairs."

"Oh," Otto wheezed. And then he made a totally unexpected offer. "You could have some of my old suits if you're interested."

I caught the glint in the old man's eye. Sensing I had the edge by providing that moment of laughter earlier in the interview, I came out with an impromptu barb.

"No thanks to your offer of the suits, Mr. Gunstrom. I'm afraid they'd be tight around the chest and loose around the stomach!"

There was still another awkward pause before once again Otto's laughter filled the office.

With a friendly shake of hands, I was dismissed from the interview. Once in the secretary's office I sighed with relief. I couldn't believe I'd gotten away with what I'd said.

And damned if I didn't get offered another contract containing a raise. I thought I'd be fired!

Those Memorable Student Assemblies

I continue to muse about the community college experience. Possibly it was the low pay and heavy teaching loads that engendered so much cohesiveness between my colleagues and me. Looking back, it seems there were scores of unique incidents that helped us rise above our "misery index" by laughing.

Student assemblies were held in the gym. Some of them provided lasting memories.

Mr. Amsel, the president of the college's first Board of Trustees was well loved throughout the community. A successful Swiss immigrant, he was a kindly, generous, polite, and respected icon. His guttural accent, however, was so pronounced that little of what he said in his occasional speeches to the student body could be understood. When he completed his presentations, he would bow and smile while acknowledging the hearty round of applause. Inevitably, someone in the audience would comment: "Wasn't he wonderful — but what did he say?"

At these assemblies (mandatory for students and faculty) in the college gym, Otto Gunstrom would often hold forth. At one memorable meeting, he was determined to issue a stern warning to the students about drinking at the pub across the highway from the college. It was commonly referred to as "G building" by students and faculty, short for the Country Grove run by the Galata family.

Campus buildings were traditionally named after the pioneers who were instrumental in getting the campus built. Large gold letters identified Gunstrom Hall, Higlee Hall, Long Hall, Husson Hall, Amel Hall, Morin Library, etc. It was rumored that whenever the agenda of the Board of Trustees meeting was light—or boredom set in—the old guys would up and name a building or two after each other. It seemed like a good way to spend the time.

For student class scheduling purposes (and since confusing the names of the buildings was so easy), the buildings were designated as A, B, C, D. There was also an E and an F and an H. But no one on campus dared tamper with the letter G. No campus structure would ever dare be called "G building." There was only one of those, and it served beer across the highway!

Otto, however, wasn't in touch with what the rabble called the Country Grove. "G Building" meant absolutely nothing to him. He only knew that the place was run by the Galatas and that it should be off limits to the students.

And so he held forth at this particular assembly condemning the mighty sin of drinking before and between classes. He worked himself into a lather, relating horror stories of staggering, sleeping in class, throwing up. He wound up his tirade with this threat: "Any student who finds his or her way to Galata's before or between classes shall immediately be suspended from attending classes!"

The only trouble was that no one in the audience recognized what *Galata's* referred to. Not a soul connected the name of the owners with good old "G Building," and so the entire tirade went right over their heads.

Otto felt that the assemblies should contain an element of spirituality and patriotism. He insisted that the college chaplain should lead all in prayer. He also insisted that all rise and sing the "Star Spangled Banner," accompanied by the college's electric organ. This was a rite that, more often than not, resulted in disaster. The national anthem is difficult enough to sing, let alone having a student, selected at the last minute from the attendees, as organ accompanist wandering awkwardly through the piece, often backtracking to correct mistakes, and varying the key with impunity.

On one particular occasion, it seemed that the entire assemblage was hopelessly bogged down in the middle of the national anthem as an embarrassed student organist struggled along, flailing at the keys and sweating profusely.

The attendees sang what notes they could recognize. It was a mess. Mercifully, it eventually came to an end.

Throughout the debacle, I was able to stifle my mirth. It wasn't easy. I lost control however when a lovely instructor from the Dental Hygiene department remarked with total sincerity, "Gee, I've never heard it done quite that way before!"

The Downfall of the Autocrat

It wasn't any secret that Hudson College's faculty received minimum pay compared with other two-year units across the state. At statewide conferences, salary was often on the informal agenda. This was a very sore topic across campus, since nothing could be done about it.

About even this, Otto was a sly fox. He had his minions among the faculty. Good old veteran Frank LaParra would start a rumor every year just after contracts were distributed. When a disgruntled employee would complain about the miserly raise offered, Frank would authoritatively offer assurance with these words: "Don't worry about it now. I know from reliable sources that we will be getting a bonus in the fall." This simply wasn't true, but it managed to reduce the complaints temporarily. It took me four years of these assurances to realize that Frank was a mole for the administration.

Otto was clever in yet another way. After the contracts were mailed out, he would leave the campus for a two-week vacation in his hometown some three hundred miles away. Infuriated faculty would storm his office only to be told he wouldn't be back for some time. Still another ploy to smooth the waters, and it worked.

Inevitably a form of organized resistance developed. The faculty union was not voted in until the 1970s, but its forerunner was the Professional Improvement Committee, a group that President Gunstrom distrusted. Bob McCaffrey became chairman of this committee in the year that it was decided to conduct a comprehensive study of community college salaries statewide from top to bottom, administration to custodial services. Since such information is public, it wasn't difficult to gather the data. The time-consuming part was organizing the comparisons.

Once that was done, the crap hit the fan. When the results became known, campus-wide shock and fury ensued. It was bad enough to see in print that the faculty were the lowest paid in the state, but it was even more infuriating to see that Otto V. Gunstrom was the highest paid two-year college president!

McCaffrey and the committee presented the salary comparison findings to the president, who considered such a study to be nothing short of treason! It shocked him to the core. His reaction: a deep draw on his cigarette before moving his head from side to side while commenting, "This is dynamite!" over and over again.

Unsurprisingly, Otto V. Gunstrom suffered a debilitating heart attack not long after being presented with the results of the salary study. He retired.

CHAPTER FOUR—UNIQUE TEACHING COLLEAGUES

When I started teaching at Hudson College, there were approximately 1,000 enrolled students. Consequently there were only a few dozen faculty. We worked together and came to know each other quite well. Since Otto Gunstrom was such an autocrat, the faculty bonded even more closely because of the mutual distaste for the autocratic manner in which we were treated. The community college expanded rapidly over the years, and inevitably close contact among the faculty was lost. Many left for better paying jobs, and newer faculty arrived on campus in droves during the '60s and '70s. We certainly had our fair share of characters, several of whom left indelible memories.

Rocco Arsini—Accounting Faculty

In the third year on the new campus, Dean Adam Collers of the School of Business hired Rocco Arsini as accounting professor. He was an extremely compulsive man who seemed obsessed with his claim of descent from Italian nobility. To him, this seemed important.

Rocco boasted that he took four or five showers a day. He washed his hands continuously. He lived in a bachelor apartment that he just knew was under siege, and he would relate the steps he took to catch the imagined culprit. Items in his bureau drawer would be arranged in such a way that any change in position would be easily detected. He'd also seal a small slip of paper in the door when he closed it behind him after leaving the apartment, so that if an intruder opened the door, the slip of paper would drop to the floor unnoticed.

Interestingly enough, Rocco was an excellent classroom teacher who earned the students' praise. That's how he managed to last two years instead of one.

Bob McCaffrey liked to relate his most indelible recollection of mercurial Rocco: "I was counseling this student who was having trouble getting along with his classmates. Since there was no other place for privacy, I had scheduled the boy to meet with me in my office, which I shared with crazy Rocco and mild-mannered Pat Pamino, another accounting professor.

"For some reason that day, Rocco seemed to be more uptight than usual. While I was advising my charge about what steps he had to take to improve his relationships, the phone rang. Pat Pamino, busily involved in preparing a test, asked in a most pleasant way if Rocco would please answer the phone."

"I'm not answering that f——— phone for you or anyone else, you son of a bitch!" Rocco shouted, jumping up from behind his desk. "I'm sick of your shit, and I'm not going to take any more of it. If you want to fight about it, let's just step out of the office!"

Pat was a nice guy but he wasn't a doormat. Out of his chair he sprang, fists doubled. "I'm ready whenever you are!' he declared."

"All of this while I was trying to guide my student toward better behavior patterns. The kid, sensing what was coming, bolted from the office. I took my life in my hands by stepping between Rocco and Pat and was able to persuade them to back down."

Stu Nimas—Business Faculty

Professor Stu Nimas, a heavy set, graying blowhard, was hired to teach Management classes. He'd commute back and forth to his home in New Hampshire on weekends.

This man would attempt to overwhelm any conversational partner with all of the latest buzzwords. "Solving that problem won't take any time at all," he was prone to assure a colleague. "All it would take is to apply a little vector analysis and some matrix theory."

Whatever that meant.

The students, however, were not bedazzled by all of Stu's ramblings. During his lectures, Stu would sprinkle in endless anecdotes about his days as a paratrooper. The war stories never ended.

The kids called him Colonel Ripcord. He was let go after the first year.

Lee Dunham—Chemistry Faculty

Lee Dunham of the chemistry department was let go because he guaranteed a young female student a better grade if she would just step into the storage closet with him for a few minutes. He was asked to clear out his desk by the end of the day.

Evelyn Karlstad—Secretarial Faculty

Evelyn Karlstad, an aging first-year secretarial teacher, left a lasting impression when she appeared at her office wearing a fur coat—right into the summer months.

She had her own brand of paranoia. The other secretarial teachers went out of their way to befriend this peculiar woman. Admiring the variety of perfumes Evelyn would wear during the week, teaching colleague Elly Flemmer inquired into the name of the manufacturer.

"I can't tell you right now," Evelyn said. "You see, I have them coded by number. After I buy them I remove the labels from the perfume bottles and then number them. I keep the manufacturers' names indexed in a miniature file cabinet which I keep in a safe in my home."

"I think I understand," was all Elly could think to say. She never again inquired.

Although her contract was not renewed, Evelyn didn't go away. She returned to the campus over and over again, year after year, wearing her fur coat while continuously working with her portable file box. I waved to her in the parking lot as she sat in the back of her car one late afternoon, industriously filing away. Several months later I found her in an empty darkened classroom, busily managing her files. No one seems to know what happened to Evelyn. She just drifted away.

Bob McCaffrey—Economics Professor

Bob McCaffrey started teaching at the college one year after I started my career there. He and I maintained a friendship that lasted some 50 years and more.

I admired Bob's quick wit, and Bob appreciated my brand of humor. We continuously ribbed each other about nationality backgrounds as well as religious affiliations. Bob was as Irish as anyone could be, and my ancestral background was Dutch. Without stretching the imagination very far, both of us could find something unkind so say about genetic idiosyncrasies. And, of course, there were those countless incidents that came up as our lives progressed at the college.

The Premature Death Conversation

It wasn't long before the faculty, who were at first few in number, cemented relationships, so much so that we began to socialize outside of class. Evenings together at a nearby pizza and beer restaurant were a treat, and the ensuing conversations were sometimes priceless.

On one occasion, four couples had a discussion about what would happen if our spouse were to pass away at a young age. The usual lamentations were expressed, but when it was Bob McCaffrey's turn, his wife, Frances, took over. Frances was bright as a whip, and boy, was she fun to be with. Both of the McCaffreys were devout Roman Catholics.

"If I was to die, I'm sure that Robert (they always addressed each other by their full first names) would wait to remarry until he'd received a special dispensation from the Pope. Not me, I'd get married again just like that," she said, snapping her fingers.

Bob immediately responded, "That's because you've had a happier marriage than I have, Frances." It brought down the house.

Student Riots across the Nation

In the midst of the Viet Nam war, students on college campuses across the country began to protest against the war. Protests turned into confrontations, which led to tragedies. One such was the unexpected incidents that occurred at Kent State University in Ohio, where several student rioters were fatally gunned down by the National Guard.

The Kent State news caused a buzz throughout the Hudson College campus. My colleagues and I entered into discussions with mixed reactions.

McCaffrey was ultra-conservative through and through. He had no sympathy at all with the rioters. When he came into the faculty office he declared: "Well, they finally did the right thing at Kent State. I think they ought to shoot a dozen students on every campus in the country!"

The absurdity of the suggestion just about staggered me. At first I wanted to shout Bob down, even though we were very close friends. Instead, I decided to desensitize such a ridiculous comment. In a calm voice I cautioned, "No, Bob, I don't think that would be fair. Why not shoot just a few students on the smaller campuses, and lots more on the larger ones." Even McCaffrey caught the humor and dropped the subject.

Harvard on the Hudson

Union Negotiations

In the '70s, the faculty formed a union. Since the pay scale at the college was the lowest for comparable institutions across the state, a faculty union was inevitable. For some time, the administration caved in to faculty demands at contract negotiations, but eventually the tide turned.

McCaffrey was on the faculty negotiating team in the early '80s. One of the most contentious issues was class size. In the past, the union had been successful in maintaining a maximum class size of 25 students. The administration pushed to raise the class size to a maximum of 33, which would save considerably on faculty salaries by reducing the number of class sections to be taught.

The opposing sides wrangled for hours and hours over this issue.

Once, the issue came up in one of the faculty offices. McCaffrey interjected, "At one point, I wanted to tell the administration's negotiating attorney that class size really didn't make much difference to me, because I can put 33 students to sleep just as easily as I can 25. But I didn't dare say it out loud."

The Economics Lesson

Professor McCaffrey had a policy of testing his Economics students early, just to see how much they grasped the subject matter. One grade by a blank-staring newcomer caught his attention: a score of 11 out of a possible 100!

McCaffrey made an appointment to have the student stop to see him in his office.

"Let's see just how much you understand about what we have covered in Economics so far," he began. We'll start with the GNP. Do you know what I'm referring to?

The student's response was "Huh?"

McCaffrey tried to make things easier. "I'm talking about the Gross National Product."

The student responded, "The what?"

"I said the Gross National Product. That's the sum total of all of the economic activity in the United States."

Another "Huh?"

"I'm going to give you an example of how the Gross National Product works. Let's put it this way: If you go to a barber and get your haircut and pay $10, that contributes $10 to the Gross National Product. Do you understand that?"

The student stared at McCaffrey for several seconds, obviously turning the conversation over in his mind. Then he uttered incredulously, "Are you trying to tell me that the barber don't get nothin'?"

With that, McCaffrey knew that he had his work cut out for him.

Harvard on the Hudson

Joe Keegan—Economics Faculty

Joe Keegan was nice guy but he was also a full-blown nervous wreck. He was so high-strung that he made others tense. As colleague McCaffrey would say, "Joe would make a cup of coffee nervous." So high-strung was Joe that in conversation he would ask questions and then answer them himself before waiting for a response. Upon approaching him in the hall, I once remarked, "Hi, Joe, how's it going?"

The staccato response: "Great Bill. Isn't it a great sunny day? It sure is. Have you talked with McCaffrey lately? I did yesterday. He's some character." No need for me to say a word. Joe could make a potential dialog into a monologue without trying.

On one occasion, I was working quietly in my office when Joe burst in.

"Bill, is it alright if I use your phone? Thanks. It won't take long. I just want to call my wife." I nodded assent. I couldn't help but hear the conversation from Joe's end of the line: "Hello, Mary, how are you doing? (No time for a response.) Great. Mary, do you want me to pick up Sally when she gets out of school? (Again no pause.) I'll take care of it. What are we having for supper? Stuffed peppers, I hope. What time will you be getting home from work? I'll see you there at five o'clock." Click went the receiver. Mary hadn't been able to say a word. Joe dashed out the door, late for class as usual. Amazing!

To the students, Joe was legendary. In class he'd pace endlessly, blinking his eyes and adjusting his glasses by pushing them up on his nose. During a lecture, he would occasionally walk out of the classroom door, proceed briskly to the water fountain, take a quick sip, and return to the classroom without pausing in his delivery.

Most memorable was his continuous fidgeting—rolling chalk in his palm, shuffling papers, jingling change in his pockets—anything to have something to do with his hands. He would hold his hard-covered binder (in which he kept his notes) in his hands and unclasp and clasp the binder clips without even knowing he was doing it.

Then came the time when a colleague was casually watching Joe's performance from outside the opened classroom door. It seems Joe, while clasping and unclasping the clips of his binder, managed to catch his necktie in the binder clasp. He tried unsuccessfully to open the clip and finally gave up, letting the binder, clinging to his tie like a crab, dangle down and swing about as he paced the floor and continued his presentation. The students looked on with amazement. Joe seemed totally unaware that something unusual was happening.

Margaret Malloy—English Comp Faculty

Margaret Malloy, in her early sixties, had dropped out as a Roman Catholic nun and had secured a job teaching English composition at the two-year college. She was from the "old school," plain attire, strict classroom discipline, and even more strict grades.

It was one of my responsibilities, after I was promoted to department chairperson of accounting, to review mid-term grades for the students in my program. For two or three semesters, I had sessions with students complaining about Margaret's grades. After assuring them of Miss Malloy's competence and fairness semester after semester, it occurred to me to look a little further into the situation.

What I found was most unsettling. Few of Margaret's students ever got as high as a "C" grade. There were many "D's" but only an occasional "A" or "B." After checking the grades of other English comp teachers, I was convinced I had to talk with Margaret. There were serious issues involving academic freedom, and then, too, I had little use for the other end of the spectrum: grade inflation. Fortunately, Margaret and I had established a great working relationship over the years. I talked to her about grading on the "normal curve". In my opinion our talk went very well with no animosity.

The after effects of our conversation, however, blew my mind. I felt I'd gotten the point across to Margaret that her grades were uncommonly severe. Never did I expect that the following semester she would do a complete turnabout by giving out only A's and B's! It took still another delicate session with Margaret before her grades followed a more normal distribution.

Jack Endres—Dental Hygiene Department Chairperson

Jack Endres was a very special guy — no-nonsense but also affable. He was previously a practicing dentist before he was advised to give it up because of high blood pressure caused by adhering to a relentless schedule of treating patients. He changed careers and became chairman of the new Dental Hygiene department at the college. His students and his faculty worshipped him. It was customary for more than 90% of the graduating seniors to pass the New York State Dental Hygiene Board exam. In some years 100% sailed through with flying colors.

Since the Business and Dental Hygiene classrooms and offices were located in the same building, it was destined that I would become fast friends with my Dental Hygiene colleagues. I truly admired Jack Endres for his professional demeanor and his self-deprecating humor.

Jack enjoyed telling this story about himself. He'd start out by saying, "Did you ever feel so damned sure of yourself that you were doing something exactly right only to screw it up so badly that you couldn't imagine what went wrong?" "That's what happened to me in the spring of 1965."

Harvard on the Hudson

"Although I love working with the young females, their annual jitters about the forthcoming state board exams used to drive me to distraction. Along about March, they would become impossible to work with. Trying to get through a class lecture was murder. Some would break into tears over nothing; others became argumentative, and each and every one of them was distracted and high-strung. "

"That spring, I decided to do something about it. I was determined to come down so hard on them that they would come to their senses and would calmly approach the May exams like adults instead of fluttering about like frightened birds."

"I carefully designed my strategy. I even practiced my brief speech over and over, just to make sure all went as planned. What I decided to do was to sternly stride into the classroom, slam down my text to get their attention, and then bellow, 'I have one thing and one thing only to say to each of you today: GROW UP!' With that I planned to turn on my heel and stomp out of the door, closing it firmly behind me."

"When the time came, everything went exactly as I planned—up to a point. The girls were in a particularly agitated state for that time of the year. Into the room I charged, slamming down my textbook on the podium. The room fell silent. Every head turned my way. Apprehensively they awaited my message. 'I have one thing and one thing only to say to each of you today,' I started, just as I had planned. And then I heard my mouth say 'GRUPPO.' The silence continued. Only this time it was due to confusion. They knew I was upset, but they had no idea what I was talking about. Neither did I. How could I possibly have said GRUPPO instead of GROW UP? I was too damned sure of myself, I guess. Boy did I get out of that room in a hurry."

Maureen Holmes—Liberal Arts Faculty

Maureen Holmes, an English professor, was extremely bright and competent. She was a favorite of the students year after year. Her reputation as a classroom teacher was so good that those faculty who had their own offspring registered at the college would make sure they were placed in Maureen's class.

Maureen loved the students. She made it a point to know them well enough to give them a break when they were experiencing temporary difficulties in their personal lives. She was known to bend the rules on attendance or on assignment deadlines if she judged that leniency was merited.

Maureen was compassionate, but she was not stupid. Students rapidly learned that she was no pushover.

Some learned the hard way — like Scott, who had chosen not to attend her English class for weeks at a time. Maureen hadn't seen Scott in class between the beginning of February and the first week in April when he unexpectedly showed up. Scott, who hadn't handed in a paper or taken a quiz since the beginning of the semester, stopped by the lectern at the close of class to ask Miss Holmes a favor.

"Miss Holmes, what will I have to do to get an 'A' in this course?"

Maureen, fixing a steady glance on the young man answered, "You could start by changing water into wine!"

Tom Hearly—Accounting Faculty

A few ex-students came back to the campus as faculty once they acquired the necessary credentials and had picked up some experience. They were often prime choices because they were a known quantity. Most of them worked out very successfully. Some were a disaster.

Such was the case with Tom Hearly. When at the college, he had proved to be bright and responsible, graduating at the top of his class. He then went on to earn advanced degrees. He served as a military officer and, following that, started a successful construction business. Unfortunately, he saw college teaching as such a breeze that he could continue to build houses while holding down a faculty position.

I had an inkling that this wouldn't work out when I invited Tom to join the accounting faculty. Tom assured me that he would cut back on the construction work if the teaching job became too demanding.

Which it did.

Tom was invariably unprepared for class. Sometimes he would show up wearing muddy construction boots and fatigues, having just climbed out of a ditch before coming to class.

Since he was a very bright person, he couldn't relate to students having difficulty with accounting, and he consequently shrugged them off as lazy or stupid.

The students began stopping at my office with complaints about Tom.

I would meet with him in an attempt to improve the situation. Tom didn't seem to grasp that there was any problem. He was simply too self-confident. By the middle of the spring semester of his first year, he was given the word that his contract would not be renewed.

Ah, but that wasn't the end of it. During his first semester at the college, Tom was assigned to teach Intermediate Accounting, a challenging course for second-year accounting majors. His office mate, Tim Hunter, another bright young faculty recruit, used to help Tom solve difficult problems, not because Tom couldn't do it himself but because he was too busy doing other things. However, faculty needed to solve problems not only to get the answer but also to be able to show the students how the problem was solved.

Harvard on the Hudson

One particularly thorny problem had taken Tim Hunter hours to solve. It involved consolidation statements.

After Tom left Hudson College, he took a teaching position at a competing private business college in the area. Coincidentally he was assigned the job of teaching Intermediate Accounting, using the exact same text as he had used at Hudson College.

One afternoon, as Tim Hunter was preparing for class, he received a phone call. The voice at the other end of the line was familiar. "Tim, this is your old buddy Tom Hearly. I've called to ask you a favor." Tim warily agreed to help out.

"Do you remember that stickler of a problem in intermediate accounting involving consolidation statements that you helped me with?"

Tim's memory clicked in. "I'm pretty sure I do."

"Well, do you think you can dig up the solution for me?' Tom asked.

"Sure, just give me some time. I'll call you back,"

Unbelievably, Tom urged, "Tim, I'm kind of in a hurry. Could you solve the problem right now? I'm in class and I just stepped away to phone you for the solution. I have to get back to the students with the answer."

Tim gently placed the receiver on the phone cradle. "Some people never change," he sighed.

Jamie Karner—Psychology Faculty

Tom Hearly wasn't the only one to wear military fatigues to class. He shared that distinction with an off-the-wall psychology teacher, Jamie Karner. Jamie, too, was extremely intelligent, and eccentric as well. She would regale those who shared a table for an occasional cup of coffee with recollections her own days as a student.

"I got this job in the library, and I was assigned to work in the stacks in the late evening hours. To relieve my boredom, I learned how to make a squeaking sound like a rat. I was quite good at it." Jamie demonstrated her remarkable talent. She was dead right about her proficiency.

"In the quiet hours, when students wandered the stacks, I would make this vermin noise, she continued. " It would scare them out of their wits!"

Jamie threw herself into the Falkland Islands controversy between England and Argentina. She became so involved that she took a leave of absence to travel to the Falklands in order to offer whatever assistance was needed. When Jamie returned to the campus, her military fatigues were her badge of courage.

Yvonne—Potential Secretarial Department Faculty

Some faculty applicants never made it through the starting gate.

Harvard on the Hudson

I was intrigued by a friend I'd met at several conferences. Yvonne was a rare bird. She smoked, dressed sloppily, didn't take care of herself, and swore a lot, but, oh, did she have a great sense of humor.

She told hilarious stories to professional colleagues about the "joys" of working in Albany's oldest business college. The place had been run for generations by a family which seemed to breed characters. The original proprietor would greet the faculty as they arrived for morning classes—stopwatch in hand and ready to dock wages for tardiness. The next generation took over and ran the place parsimoniously. The heat was turned so low in winter that Yvonne had to wear her fur-lined boots to class. She was desperately seeking a better job.

I had heard from many sources that she was an excellent teacher in spite of her earthy drawbacks. She knew a few risky jokes and often used inappropriate language. I suggested Yvonne apply for a position in the secretarial department at Hudson College. I even helped set up the interview, since the chairperson of the secretarial department was a close friend.

The chairperson, much in contrast to Yvonne, was every inch a lady. Stella Van Alken was well mannered, reserved, and always professional in conduct and appearance.

I could see a slight frown cross Stella's brow when Yvonne arrived for the interview, smoking a cigarette and plodding along in loose-fitting boots. Yvonne's casual style and gutter language, which I had at first thought amusing, immediately became a liability. The interview was over before it began.

The clincher came when Stella asked Yvonne why she was leaving her current position.

"That cheap old bastard that runs the business college offered me a contract with a salary that was so low I barely could afford to eat. So I told him to shove it up his ass!"

Stella grimaced. "We'll be contacting you in the near future," she assured Yvonne, showing her to the door.

"And just where did you find that piece of work?" Stella asked me, her voice dripping with ice.

Dina Lockart—Food Service Department Chairperson

Dina Lockhart was hired to chair the new Food Services Department. She was crammed into one office with four other chairpersons including Stella and me. It was hell on privacy and disastrous for student advisement, but all of the chairs got along extremely well. We laughed a lot, particularly after Dina was added to the mix.

Dina had her share of frustrations. For one thing, the president of the college didn't like her. It probably started when she had her class bake a generous supply of cookies, on one of which the president broke his tooth.

Dina would share stories of her travails. While Stella usually held her reserve, Dina had a way of breaking through that shield in a way that few others could. When she told her stories with Stella present, I would sit back in amazement waiting for Stella to shut down the conversation.

"Yesterday I asked the class to bake butter pecan cookies," Dina related on one occasion, trying to stifle herself from laughing too hard to complete the story. "I always go from student to student, checking their progress. As I stopped by one kid, he asked me what I thought of his cookies. I answered, "I think your nuts are too big!" With that the kid said, 'Gee, thanks, Mrs. Lockart. No one ever told me that before.'" Stella laughed so hard that she had to put her head down on her desk.

And then there was Dina's story about Barbara Pickens, chairperson of the Biology Department. Barbara was as professional and meticulous as anyone could possibly be. Her clothes were tailor made, and every hair was always in place. She seldom smiled. And, like so many chairpersons in science departments, she occupied a well-appointed, spacious office with a grand view of the campus.

Dina had made an appointment to meet with Barbara in her luxurious office. When she returned to the cramped warren occupied by five business chairpersons, she commented to all, "Jesus, have you guys ever seen Barbara Pickens' office? You could get laid in there and no one would know the difference!"

I was sure Stella would storm out of the office. Wrong again. She was daubing her eyes with tissue to mop the tears of laughter cascading down her cheeks.

Clarence Hogle—Business Professor

Clarence Hogle was ill suited to become a community college business teacher. He was a gentleman in his forties who had good manners, refined demeanor, and a fine head of silvering hair which, for some reason, he died to a bluish hue. Previous to his arrival on the business division faculty at the Hudson College, he had served as an admissions director at two women's colleges. He just wasn't prepared for our caliber of student.

Clarence had a fine sense of humor, a clever mind — and a serious drinking problem. He lived with his ageing mother and his dog, Ginger, in a flat not far from the college. Somehow, he and I became fast friends, probably because I wanted to help him adjust to the community college atmosphere and because I knew Clarence was a lonely man.

This friendship carried beyond the college. Since Clarence was lonely, he would ask me to be his luncheon companion at a restaurant off campus. This sometimes involved a "three martini" lunch, which Clarence insisted upon paying for. After a few of these treats, I sensed that it was habit forming and cut back on accepting the invitations. After the fun-filled luncheons, Clarence could go home and take a nap. I, however, often had late afternoon classes, and teaching a class while glazy-eyed was problematic to say the least.

The admonition to the children

On holidays from the college, my wife, Sandy, would ask me to invite Clarence for an overnight. He was good company, and he was lonely. Clarence would readily accept. A few years after Clarence came to the community college, his mother, to whom he was deeply attached, passed away. A few months later, his beloved dog, Ginger, also passed on. Clarence was devastated. When the Christmas recess came about, Sandy had me invite Clarence to our home. At the time we were living in relatively cramped quarters with our three offspring: Mark, age 4; Grant, 3; and Jennifer, 1. The boys slept in bunk beds, and Jennifer was in a crib. In preparation for bedtime, the boys were to share the top bunk, and Clarence was to take the bottom one.

Before Clarence arrived, I had admonished each of the boys not to mention Clarence's mother or his dog, because they had gone to be with God and Clarence missed them dearly. Mark and Grant gravely nodded their heads with understanding.

Things went awry very early the next morning. Just as dawn arrived, I heard Grant (who had a lisp at that age) trying to awaken Mr. Hogle. After a few tries, Clarence grunted. At that point, Grant said, "Misther Hogle, do you mind if I asthk you a question?" Clarence again grunted. "Misther Hogle, do you think your dog, Ginger, isth up in heaven with your mother?"

That was precisely what he was told *not* to do. "Well, he got both the mother and the dog in one sentence," I commented to Sandy.

The Dinty Moore Stew incident

Sometimes the students were downright cruel to Clarence. Behind his back, they made fun of his bluish hair and also the way he carried his books close to his chest instead of at his side. His discipline was lax because he just wasn't able to handle some of the raucous students. On one occasion, a student with a thermos full of Dinty Moore stew hidden under his shirt, rose and declared. "Mr. Hogle, I don't feel good. Can I please go to the men's room?" Clarence, unaware of the ruse, gave permission. With that the student arose and walked up to the front of the room. As he passed the lectern, he faked a vomiting spell and simultaneously crushed the thermos to his chest, spilling its contents on the floor. The class roared. Clarence left the room in disgust.

Student-parent night

For some years, the college had a student-parent night on which parents were invited to come to the campus to meet their student's classroom professor. Of course, the parents came along for the main purpose of talking about their offspring's academic progress. One evening, the parents of one of the worst students, Bill Jones, arrived filled with concern.

They expressly asked to see Clarence, who happened to be in his office. The Dean went to Clarence's office and told him the Joneses had arrived and wanted to speak to him. The invitation to meet with the parents was turned down flatly by Clarence, who said, "Their son is a dolt, and I have no intention of discussing it with them." That was that!

The Last Straw

Clarence drank heavily — vodka martinis with a twist. At the very young age of 57 he was incapable of continuing to meet classes. I overheard the phone call the Dean made to Clarence, who was at home and had not appeared to proctor the final exam for his course. The Dean was most irritated. His fingers jabbed at the phone dial. The phone rang and rang and rang. Finally Clarence answered in a very weak voice. He was suffering from a terrible hangover.

"Clarence, where are you?" the Dean shouted into the phone. "Don't you realize that you are supposed to be here proctoring your final exam?"

Clarence answered feebly, "Let me check my schedule. He apparently left the phone off the hook and never came back to answer it.

The Dean kept shouting "Clarence!" over and over into the phone but was met with dead silence.

Within the month, Clarence was relieved of his duties on the basis of poor health. He died a few weeks after being let go.

Amy Kendall—Phys Ed and Liberal Arts Chairperson

Over the years, Amy Kendall and I developed a close friendship. Since both of us were chairpersons at the college, we attended endless meetings together and eventually formed a close bond.

There was to be a meeting in the administrative building somewhat distant from the main campus, so far away, in fact, that attendants had to drive to the location across the highway from the campus. The meeting was scheduled after classes on what turned out to be a hot, late spring day. I had chosen to drive my 1931 Model A Ford to college that day and was totally dismayed to find that it had a flat tire when I arrived in the parking lot.

Flat tires on the Model A were not rare. I'd been driving the damned car for thirty years, and changing tires had become routine. Spare tires were mounted on the front fenders, which made the chore easier. The job involved jacking up the car, removing the wheel lugs, etc. Not a fun effort, particularly when I was running late for the chairpersons' meeting. No way to avoid it, however, so I got started. I even had an old blanket in the rumble seat, which I laid down on the pavement next to the wheel. With resignation I took off my jacket and knelt down on the blanket in order to start removing the wheel lugs. I was in no mood for such an onerous task, and I undertook it begrudgingly.

While removing a lug I saw someone's shadow next to me. Scanning the individual from bottom to top, I saw dark red shoes, stockings, and a seersucker skirt and jacket. It was friend Amy Kendall.

"Is there anything I can do to help?" she asked. Frustrated, hot and tired, the last thing I needed for this one-person job was assistance. But a clever response came to mind. "You want to be helpful? Why don't you just lie down on this blanket and you and I can go at it right here in the parking lot!"

At first Amy was flabbergasted; then her sense of humor kicked in. We both had a great laugh and then Amy warned, "When you finally get to the meeting, don't you dare tell anyone what you said to me. It would be most embarrassing." I reflected on the request and agreed not to say a word.

"See you over there as soon as I get this damned wheel replaced," I said, and Amy drove her own car off to the meeting.

It took about twenty minutes to change the tire, but I finally arrived at the meeting, somewhat rumpled and dirty after the ordeal in the parking lot.

As I stepped through the room entrance, laughter erupted from my assembled colleagues. Amy apparently had reneged about keeping our parking lot conversation under wraps.

Mel Omein—Accounting Faculty

Mel was a so-so classroom teacher. He had joined the accounting faculty a few years after me, and we were good friends, even after I was promoted to become his boss. Mel, who always seemed older than his age, was quiet, bespeckled, balding, and had an Arabic nose— a mild-mannered guy who also happened to have an eye for the ladies. I was told he carried a small black book that contained a list of possible conquests. Every so often, he would leave early after classes for pursuits unknown.

Boy, did I get in trouble one time when his wife phoned our office and I answered.

"This is Valerie Omein and I'd like to speak to my husband, Mel."

"He's not here, Valerie. I believe he's left for the day."

"How come he left so early — what is his schedule?"

I gave her a detailed report of Mel's office hours and when his classes were scheduled. Big mistake!

Harvard on the Hudson

The following day, Mel stormed into my office, obviously upset. "I don't want you ever to give anyone my schedule, especially my wife." He stormed out, slamming the door behind him. From then on my lips were sealed.

The years passed, and it came time for Mel to retire. At that time, there was a mandatory retirement age of 72, which was later ruled illegal due to age discrimination.

Mel was approaching 72, and he didn't want to retire. His home life was an unhappy one, and he had little interest in anything other than his job.

The student complaints became an avalanche with every passing week. The main concern was Mel's deafness. Students would ask him questions in class, and he simply couldn't hear them. The faulty hearing progressed rapidly, and something had to be done. Since Mel was approaching retirement age rapidly as well, the dean and I agreed that the best solution would be to have him wind up his career at the college.

I got the job of breaking the news to him.

He was invited into my office at a time when no one else was around, and we began our private conversation.

"Mel, we have been together a long time, but I think it's time you considered retirement," I began.

He became incensed. Retirement was the last thing on his mind.

"This really upsets me," he declared. "Why are you suggesting that I retire?"

I told him about the mounting number of student complaints that were coming in to me and other faculty on a daily basis. They had been coming in by the dozens.

"Specifically, what are they complaining about?" he demanded to know.

"They say you have a serious hearing problem. They say they put up their hand to ask a question and that you ignore them. They say you are very deaf!"

With that, Mel incredulously cupped his hand behind his ear and said, "*WHAT?*"

After that, Mel made an appointment with an audiologist and was told that his deafness had progressed to the extent that little could be done. With that expert opinion under his belt, Mel retired.

CHAPTER FIVE—SOME UNFORGETTABLE STUDENTS

The Community College Movement

The community college movement in New York State gained momentum in the 1960s. The goal was to develop institutions of higher learning that were affordable. Originally, one-third of the cost was born by the state, one-third by the county, and one-third by the student. Technical learning was the main emphasis, although liberal arts courses were a part of the subject mix.

Since this was a new development, students had to be recruited through advertising and direct community contact by the newly hired admissions personnel, administration, and faculty. After a few years, the graduates passed the word around, and more and more students came forth as the news spread about available programs, good teaching, low cost, and possibilities for transfer to four-year institutions as well as for job opportunities.

Most of the first crop of students, however, were not the secondary school "academic achievers" a faculty member would love to have in class. Many were challenging in terms of appearance and seriousness of purpose, with the exception of the female students. There were very few of them, perhaps only two or three in a class, but for the most part they were dignified and well behaved.

It took some time for me to get used to my male classroom charges, having previously taught only female secretarial majors in high school. At Hudson College, we had a high-spirited bunch, and it was quite a balancing act to keep them in line while imparting course content.

At first, because there were so few, the students were sorted into groups of twenty-five or so. These groups followed the same schedule throughout the week. It didn't take long for the cohesion to take place. Particularly when it came to cheating.

Cheating

I knew enough to keep my eyes peeled and my ears alert, but some of the guys were truly adept. There would be foot tapping and knocks on the desk—code signals that the military would have envied. They would change seating arrangements to be closer to confederates. They passed notes stealthily.

On one occasion, a clean-cut, athletic-looking young man literally turned his head around, looking behind him in an attempt to read his colleague's answers. I was right on his case. "Cunningham, what are you trying to do?" I inquired. Cunningham shot back an ingenious reply, "Just smelling my shoulder, Mr. Stevens."

"Smelling your shoulder!" I loudly exclaimed, commanding the class's attention and getting a good laugh from the group.

At the end of the semester, when all of the cheating damage was done, I would join the group after class at the bar across the street to find out exactly what cheating methods worked the best. This valuable information could be used when monitoring future tests. Since the grades were in, the students had nothing to lose by divulging their methods. One young man, Elmer, proudly announced that he always wore a sport coat on test day. That way he could sneak notes into the breast pocket and cleverly read them by adjusting his shoulders. Another, Phil, wrote answers on his hands and lower arms. To Robin, three taps by his pen on the desk meant he was seeking the answer to the third question. They may not have been very bright, but they sure were clever.

How to Spell "Be Able"

One outgoing young student, Tom O'Connell, was a typical young man from the nearby area of south Troy. He would argue about his test and writing scores if he thought he might have the slightest chance of changing my mind. On one of his essays, he misused the words "be able" as one combined word "beable" throughout the exercise.

When I handed back the essays, O'Connell's was the first hand to go up. "Mr. Stevens, what's wrong with the word "beable?" I patiently explained that he should have made it two words instead of one.

O'Connell wouldn't let it go. He argued on and on, giving several examples of where he thought "beable" was one word. O'Connell thought he sounded convincing, but even his classmates shook their heads in dismay. He finally gave up.

A Way to Deal with Student Discontent over Grades

My teaching colleague, Charlie Meehar, had perfected a way of dealing with students who questioned the way they were graded on a particular test question. He would politely say, "I can see why you may have interpreted the question the way you did; but, nevertheless, the grade stands. I'm not going to change it,"

The Polite but Ever-so-persistent Sikh

As the years passed, "Harvard on the Hudson" as Hudson College was dubbed by some students, accepted increasing numbers of students from other nations. Most were very capable, and some were polite almost to the point of being obsequious.

Harvard on the Hudson

Ahmed was a Sikh from India, aged somewhere in his thirties or forties. He invariably wore a maroon-colored turban. He had some difficulties in my class because of the difficulty he was having adjusting to the English language. While I was sympathetic to his plight, there were levels of proficiency that had to be met.

I dreaded returning a test paper to Ahmed. Invariably he would appear at my office after class, begging for a grade increase. He would put his hands together and bow several times, then start his practiced routine.

"Mr. Stevens, you are very good man and excellent teacher. I know I got a "C" on my test, but could you make it "B" please?" I would repeat over and over why I couldn't raise the grade. This happened every time, test after test. Finally, it occurred to me how to solve the problem. On the next test, when Ahmed deserved a firm "C," I gave him a "D." After class came the same routine, with Ahmed bowing and begging: "Mr. Stevens, I know I deserve the "D," but could you make it "C" please. I hemmed and hawed and finally agreed to raise the grade to a "C" (the grade Ahmed deserved in the first place) just to have peace. This pleased Ahmed no end—he had won a bargain. And so I followed the same procedure for the rest of the semester.

W. L. Staats

Donna at the Adult Theater

Part of the treat of teaching and advising was getting to know some of the students more intimately than others, mainly the ones who were bright and interesting—and fun. Donna didn't follow the community college mold. She was in her late thirties, but she fit in well with her classmates, most of whom were younger.

Donna and I once had a memorable conversation over lunch with several other students from her class at the pub across the road from "Harvard on the Hudson." She told of her experiences as a ticket seller at an adult movie house in Albany.

"One time," she related, "I was selling tickets, and this very old couple arrived at the ticket window."

"I don't think you want to go to see this movie," Donna warned them.

"We have our money and we're going in," came the response from the elderly lady, somewhere in her late 70s or early 80s."

"But look at the other people buying tickets. None of them are older folks. You would not be at ease here. I guarantee it," Donna told the old woman.

But the aged potential customer persisted. "We are adults and we have every right to go into an adult theater."

Harvard on the Hudson

Donna gave it another shot, "Look at the title of the movie. It's called 'Deep Throat.' Do you really think you'll enjoy that movie?"

"Give us our tickets. Here's the money. We're going in!!" the elderly wife insisted. All this time, her husband stood by, saying nothing.

In they went.

About fifteen minutes later, the old lady came storming out of the theater and made a beeline to Donna's ticket window. "Call the police!" she demanded. "Do you have any idea what is going on in that movie?" On and on she raved about the sin and sex.

Curiously enough, however, her elderly husband never came out of the movie house.

Steve with the Temper

He seemed like a nice guy when in class. Quiet, sturdily built, polite, good-looking, but not that competent when it came to his performance in my accounting class. Steve stuttered, and that must had an influence on his being quiet. He carried a high "D" in the course, and desperately needed a "B" on his final exam to raise his average to an acceptable "C" in order to meet graduation requirements.

It didn't happen. He failed the final dismally.

A few days after the final grades were sent out, his mother phoned me in the late afternoon. The college had emptied out since classes were just about over. I was finishing up another day as Acting Dean of the School of Business.

"I'm Steve Loken's mother. My son has a terrible temper," she began and then went on to say that Steve had received his final grades and was taking the results very badly. "He broke a kitchen chair and tipped over the refrigerator. Then he ran out of the house and drove off in his car. Mr. Stevens, I'm afraid he's headed in your direction, and I just wanted to warn you!"

I thanked her for her call and put down the receiver.

What to do?

After musing for a while, I phoned the college security office and asked them to send over a security guard just in case Steven showed up and was bent on revenge.

I couldn't believe my eyes when the guard appeared at my office door. There stood a shriveled 75-year-old who looked like he needed a good rest more than anything else. He was stooped over and couldn't have weighed more than 80 pounds.

Some protection!

I thanked the guard for coming over, put on my jacket, and left the office for the day.

Harvard on the Hudson

The Terrorist

I am a coward.

It was back in '60s when all hell broke loose on college campuses across the country. Students were protesting the Viet Nam war. At Kent State in Ohio, the National Guard had over-reacted and fatally shot several students.

In news photos, ominous looking young men, sometimes labeled as terrorists, were arming themselves and wearing bandoliers across their chests, taking over Dean's offices and harassing college administrators. There was a compelling photograph of a bearded, frightening-looking rioter in fully armed regalia as he took over an office at Cornell University. It was splashed across newspaper headlines in nationwide circulations.

While Hudson College was relatively peaceful, everyone was aware of potential student eruptions. I had kept up on the TV news and had been reading the political developments with intense interest.

1968-69 was the year in which I had agreed to act as Dean of the School of Business in the absence of my boss, who had taken a leave of absence to assume the job as mayor of the city of Troy. My days as an administrator were filled with increasing demands for written reports and endless meetings.

I much preferred working directly with students in a teaching and advisory capacity, but I had agreed to take the temporary job, and sometimes it kept me at my desk into the late afternoons and evenings.

One very late afternoon I was in my office. Few classes were scheduled at that time, and the college corridors were ominously quiet.

Suddenly, my office door opened, and there stood a tall, broad-shouldered, swarthy, bearded, and menacing-looking student.

I was positive that this unexpected intrusion was the first step in a campus takeover. I became hyper. Trembling, I stood up and said to the student in a quavering voice, "What do you want?"

The student was completely taken back by my frightened reaction, "I came in to see if you had a pencil sharpener I could use. We're having a test in the classroom across the hall and yours was the closest office, so I just stepped in." Then the student asked, "Are you gonna' be OK?"

This Acting Dean of the School of Business was red-faced with embarrassment.

Ghada

A mature Egyptian student, Ghada, was enchanting, sultry, somewhat devious, and very persistent. I took a liking to her because she was so bright, and I was able to learn so much more about her native country when we chatted outside of class.

Ghada was one persistent lady. So persistent that I was amazed that my secretary, Ella, remained so calm and accommodating when it came to computerizing Ghada's schedule of subjects each semester. Ghada would spend endless minutes developing the schedule with Ella as other students patiently waited in line to set up their own course times.

Once finished, Ghada would thank Ella profusely for her time and then go out into the hallway to consult with her friends about her schedule. One friend didn't like the math teacher Ghada had been scheduled for, so she returned to Ella to take more time changing her schedule.

"Where do you ever get the patience to deal with Ghada?" I inquired of Ella.

"Oh, she's all right, Mr. Stevens," Ella replied. "Ghada just needs understanding and a little guidance."

One hot day in late spring, when students were setting up their fall schedule, Ghada had come into the office repeatedly to change her schedule.

I was aware of this since Ella was visible in her outer office. Underneath her calm exterior, however, the pot was beginning to boil over. Her office was hot and stuffy, and the task of continuously trying to satisfy some of the more demanding students, like Ghada, was wearing her down.

Not long after their conversation, Ghada reappeared at Ella's desk. This time she wasn't happy with the timing of a late afternoon class and wanted it changed.

The volcano erupted.

"Out, Ghada, out!" Ella screamed, pointing to the door. "I've had it with you! Either accept the schedule we've worked over for the fourth time today, or find someone else to help you! *Out!*" Ghada knew when to hit the road and she vanished without hesitation.

The Tipsy Student

Susan Dodson was a pretty, petite, quiet student in class who seldom contributed to any part of discussions except when called upon. On one occasion, however, her Jekyl/Hyde characteristic emerged.

We were going over math test grades. Those were the days when it didn't seem harmful to read aloud students' grades while in the process of returning the test.

Apparently, Susan had some free time before the late afternoon class, and she had decided to spend the time enjoying some beers at the pub across the street from the college. Unbeknownst to me, she was smashed!

Harvard on the Hudson

Her problem soon evidenced itself when I began handing back the tests and reading off the grade as I did so.

"Al Phillips, you got a 'B' this time," I announced.

That's when this unexpected voice from my sweet, petite, young lady burst out loudly, "Go Al. I knew you could do it!" she said.

After that unsettling outburst, I read off the next grade. "Mary, your grade is an 'A'."

Again came the inebriated voice, "Yay, Mary, good for you!"

I absorbed that comment without giving a response even though I was becoming uneasy.

"Greg, you had a problem this time around. You only received a 'D.'"

Again the voice from Susan in the back of the room, "Shame on ya', Greg!"

I couldn't hold back any longer. "Susan, it would better all around if you just remained silent," I admonished.

Then I proceeded to give back the next test. "Peter, you managed to pass this one with a 'C.' Congratulations!"

"Way to go, Peter," glazy-eyed Susan chimed in.

That was it for me. The last straw.

"Susan, I think it best if you left the room. I look forward to seeing you at our next class session—with a clearer head!" Problem solved.

George Yee, the Minority Student

George Yee was a Chinese student in his teens. Like so many Asians he studied hard and was at the top of his class academically. Since I was teaching math, I truly enjoyed having such a competent student. Not only that, George had a friendly, outgoing manner, and he responded well to kidding.

One time, when the hall was relatively empty, I saw George sitting outside of a classroom with his back against the wall waiting for the bell to ring so that he could go to his next class.

Feeling chipper and knowing that George would take it well, I greeted him with the observation, "George, how does it feel to be a minority?"

Without hesitation George responded, "A minority, Mr. Stevens? Do you know that there are two billion of us? How can I be a minority?" Both of us enjoyed the banter.

Harvard on the Hudson

Bill in La-La Land

The '60s were a time never to be forgotten: Women's rights, Viet Nam War protests, The Great Society, Civil Rights, Woodstock—and drugs, drugs, drugs.

The worst of it all was the drugs. Timothy Leary accelerated it all, and the wreckage done to individuals, families, friends, and society was immeasurable. And still it continues: physical and mental impairment, theft, arson, and even murder.

It was a most fascinating decade in which to be a college professor and student advisor.

One of my advisees was a young man from Massachusetts named Bill Bixby. Although bright and personable, his behavior was erratic. He would cut classes for days and days at a time. I was talking to him about this when he shared this bit of information. "You know, Mr. Stevens, sometimes I have a little LSD and go to a particular cliff in the Berkshire Mountains near my home. Mr. Stevens, when I'm high, I can stare at a blade of grass and literally watch it grow before my eyes." I often wonder what happened to Bill after he dropped out of college. What a waste!

The Class of 1965-67—The Carburetor Incident

Probably the most interesting group of students in my recollections was the Business Administration majors from 1967-69. In those days, the students were assigned to sections of twenty-five and took all of their classes as unified group. I taught them Math of Finance. There was almost instant chemistry among the twenty-five once they got to know each other. Following graduation from Hudson College several of the group transferred to the University at Albany and from there received BS degrees.

For some forty years, about half a dozen of them have remained friends and have kept in touch with me. I attended six of their weddings and on various occasions over the years, I was invited to outings and other parties with this fun-to-be-with group.

There are several stories which have been told and retold over the decades. One involved Ernie and Don's trip out west, and it shed a light on Ernie's frugality. It seems they drove in Ernie's vintage MG across the USA. On the return trip, coming east, the car broke down outside of Tulsa, Oklahoma. Don is an excellent auto mechanic, and he rapidly diagnosed that the carburetor had a fatal flaw and had to be replaced. It was a blazing hot Sunday, and the prospect of finding an open garage was very dim. The boys trudged through the quiet, unpopulated streets seeking a garage, and lo and behold, after several hours they found one that was open. When they told the proprietor their problem, he miraculously produced the carburetor they needed. It was almost incredible to find such a part for an old, rare sports car, and to find it on a quiet Sunday morning in a deserted city!

When Ernie asked the price, he was told it would be a very modest $25. You can imagine Don's shock when he heard Ernie's answer to the quoted price. "That's way too much for what I can afford. Would you be willing to take $10?" Don was about to kill his companion, but apparently they settled the bill, returned to the MG, and went merrily on their way.

The Great Society Student Financial Assistance Program

When President Lyndon Johnson pushed through the Great Society programs in the '60s, we at the college never dreamed of some of the consequences the student-aid program would cause. When initiated, there were generous handouts by the Federal Government — with few controls.

Needy students applied for loans, and the cash rewards came easily. All one had to do was sign up as a full-time student each semester and the tuition would be paid directly to the student by check. It didn't take long for some of the more unscrupulous ones to realize that they could sign up for classes, get the money, and then drop out of the college—until the following semester when they would again sign up for classes, receive a check, and drop out. And on and on and on for succeeding semesters.

As Accounting Department advisor, I watched this waste of money go on with dismay. When one of my advisees showed up for the fourth time in two years, having dropped out three times, I resorted to sarcasm. "Instead of darkening my door, why don't you go over to the Greyhound Bus Station? They're more used to arrivals and departures than I am." It passed right over the boy's head.

Eventually, someone somewhere in authority changed the ground rules when it came to student-loan handouts. Henceforth, it became necessary for a student to have at least a "C" average in order to be eligible for additional loans.

Following the new ruling, I had a conversation with an advisee regarding his "D" average. "Mr. Powell, your unsatisfactory grades force me to recommend your academic dismissal from the accounting program.

Tears welled up in the boy's eyes. "You can't put me out!" he pleaded. "If you do, I'll have to start repaying my loans."

In addition there was the student tutoring program debacle. An office was set up to provide financial assistance to students who would serve as tutors, helping out other students who were in academic difficulty. All the floundering student had to do was get permission from his academic advisor, and he would go to the tutoring advisor and set up a schedule to meet with a peer for help.

On the surface, the objective was noble. The devil, as usual, was in the details.

Harvard on the Hudson

One of my accounting students was experiencing academic difficulties in his first- semester Principles of Accounting course. I gave him permission to go to the tutoring advisor for assistance. A week later, the student appeared in my office.

"Mr. Stevens, I think I have a serious problem. I'm in deep academic trouble in accounting and I was assigned a tutor — but I don't think the guy knows as much about accounting as I do—and I'm just about hopeless."

With that, I phoned the tutoring advisor and arranged to meet with the assigned tutor immediately. Within fifteen minutes, I met the young fellow in the tutoring lab. "Are you tutoring Accounting students?" I asked. "Oh, yeah," the young man enthusiastically replied. "I help out four or five of them!"

"Have you ever taken the Principles of Accounting course," I asked out of sheer curiosity.

"Sure I did. I got a 'D'!"

"You received a 'D' and you think you are qualified to help other accounting students? Why, that's unbelievable!" I declared.

The student's next response just about floored me. "That's nothin'. I'm tutoring other kids in Statistics and I never even took that course!"

In no time flat I contacted the tutoring administrator and was able to get the tutoring assignment rules amended.

Conversations Overheard in the Hall Between Classes

Because so many students crowded the hallways when changing classes, they raised their voices during conversations with each other. By keeping my ears peeled, I heard some most interesting comments. In one instance, I saw a few students come out of a classroom in state of anxiety. They had just completed a challenging test, and they weren't happy about it.

One young man made a most interesting statement: "I just know I flunked that test, and I blame it more on her teaching than on my studying, because I didn't study at all!" Talk about twisted logic!

In another instance, I overheard several students chatting not long after classes had resumed after the spring break. Obviously one of the dudes had been to Florida, judging from his boast: "I met this chick on the beach and she looked me over and said, "Your eyes match your bathing suit," to which I asked, "Why, because they're blue? " Oh, no," she demurely responded, "because they're bulging!"

CHAPTER SIX—THE "ENTREPRENEURS," THE BUSINESS STUDENTS' CLUB

In the mid '60s, when the student population in the Business Division had increased and the college was beginning to establish a fine academic reputation, a core of fun-loving and hard-working students evolved.

It was time to establish a club for extra-curricular activities, including guest speakers, off-campus field trips, and social outings.

In spite of my exasperating experiences with my immature high school groups, I agreed to serve as advisor to the club, which was appropriately named "The Entrepreneurs" by the Dean.

Off-campus Excursions

Our proximity to the financial center of the world, New York City, made it ideal for the bus trips that became an annual event for the Entrepreneurs for some 20 years.

My wife and I, as chaperones, used the opportunity to thoroughly explore the Big Apple where we visited ever so many places of interest. I often invited other faculty and occasionally close friends and family to partake in the excursion.

The routine was planned with the students weeks before the bus came to the campus to pick them up. The group would first visit the New York Stock Exchange, then the Federal Reserve Building, and finally the American Stock Exchange. Following that, the students would be on their own. A list of suggested activities was distributed.

According to the schedule, the bus would pick up the Entrepreneurs at the campus at 6 a.m. By 9 a.m., they would be let off the bus at the New York Stock Exchange on Wall Street. By noon, the tours of the business establishments would be completed, and the students would separate to enjoy the rest of the day. At 11 p.m. the bus would pick up the group near Radio City Music Hall, and they would travel back to Troy, arriving at 2 or 3 a.m. It was always a full day.

The New York Stock Exchange was bustling, and the experienced guides did a fine job of providing the students with information about what was going on as they overlooked the floor of the exchange from a balcony. No visitors were allowed on the floor where business transactions were taking place. Previous to seeing the exchange in action, the students were seated in a small theater for viewing a clever cartoon depicting exactly how stock transactions took place. That was great preparation. It was a terrific educational experience.

Next was the visit to the Federal Reserve Bank, where the Entrepreneurs were taken some 80 feet down from street level in an elevator to a vault where most of the gold bars in the world are stored. This was a revelation to me who thought all gold was in Fort Knox, Tennessee. Actually, the bars, weighing about 35 lbs. each, never leave the New York City underground location. When gold is transferred from, say, Saudi Arabia to England, the bars are literally taken out of the Saudi Arabia cage in New York City and put into the cage assigned to England. The students could see the gold bars in cages by standing behind a thick glass door. First, however, they had several vault doors to navigate through before viewing the awesome sight of all of that gold.

The third place of interest, the American Stock Exchange, was a few blocks from the Federal Reserve Bank. This exchange is a lot smaller than the New York Stock Exchange and much more action-oriented, with hand signals used to depict stock transactions. The guide skillfully interpreted the hand signals for us. Fascinating.

By noon the official business part of the trip ended, and the students were turned loose. I told them about the buffet restaurant where my wife and I would eat lunch and also gave them the phone number of the restaurant (there were no cell phones at the time) where we could be reached in the event that contact was necessary.

Only once did I receive a phone call from a student, and it was an incredible conversation. When I initially saw his name on the trip roster, I knew we were taking along one of the oddest individuals who had ever belonged to the club. He confirmed it when he said, "Mr. Stevens, I want you to know that I am back in Troy. I took a bus back home because I couldn't find anything to do in New York City." In New York City – Wow!

I thanked the young man for calling; at least I knew where he was. The most dreaded thing to occur on such a trip would be to have a student missing. In all of the years, we never lost track of one.

After several years of enjoying lunches at the buffet restaurant, we had to change eating locations. The last time there, we spotted a rat busily gnawing on a turkey drumstick right at the center of the buffet table. Yuk!

It never ceased to amaze my wife and me how some students wasted a day in the big city that could have given them an opportunity to do something unique, something they would remember the rest of their lives, like going to the Statue of Liberty or to the top of the World Trade Center or the Empire State Building. Or going to a live theater presentation.

We would ask the students on the bus trip home how they spent the day after the noon hour when they were set free. One girl had had her hair done. One guy had gone bowling. Couldn't they have done that at home?

Harvard on the Hudson

Sandy and I did it all: the theaters, the World Trade Center, the Empire State Building, the Natural History Museum, the Guggenheim Museum, the Metropolitan Art Museum, the Planetarium, the Fisk Museum, Fifth Avenue, Tiffany's, Macy's, Gimbles, Central Park, art galleries, the Tavern on the Green, and so much more. It was always so exciting, even when it rained.

The "Expletive" Button:

Nothing can ever duplicate Times Square. It was there where I got to deal first hand with one of the city's gruff merchants. I was walking along Broadway when I spotted a store window featuring lapel button pins with various words on them. One really attracted me. It read "Horseshit" in Old English script on a lavender background. I had to have it.

I walked into the store and said to the clerk, who immediately treated me as though I was an intruder instead of a customer, "I'd like one of those 'Horseshit' buttons."

"We don't sell 'em by name, pal. We sell 'em by number. Look in the window and get the number."

I did as directed. I went outside, looked at the window display, and noted that the pin was No. 29.

Back into the store I went. "I'd like pin No. 29!" I told the less-than-friendly clerk. Probably because the pin was only 50 cents, the clerk didn't care much about pleasing this customer. He walked over to a series of trays containing buttons, reached into one and pulled out a pin and threw it onto the counter. I saw that instead of 'horseshit' the one the clerk selected read 'bullshit. '

I said, "This isn't the pin I want. I want the one that reads 'horseshit' and you gave me one labeled 'bullshit.'"

The clerk couldn't believe his ears. He gave me an ugly stare and grumbled "horseshit — bullshit," what's the difference?"

I replied indignantly, "Horseshit is much more refined, don't you think?"

The clerk went back to the trays, grabbed a "horseshit" pin, and literally tossed it in my direction.

I left the store in a spirit of conquest. I had won!

Awaiting the bus

Since the bus would pick up the students near Radio City Music Hall, my wife and I needed an inside place to wait for it. We preferred a bar named Hurley's. We would get to the pub at 10 p.m. or so in time to have a beer or two before boarding the bus. We never told the students where we were sequestered before 11 p.m.

The other chaperones would frequently join Sandy and me for a drink or two. One time we invited two other faculty couples to join us on the bus trip. Tim Hunter and Gene Carter brought along their wives. The conversation over a beer would invariable involve the activities they had enjoyed in the free time after the field-trip visits.

The Circus:

One year we had chosen to go to Madison Square Garden to see the Ringling Brothers Circus. It turned out to be one of the most hilarious shows I had ever attended.

Toward the end of the show, an elephant was introduced as "Sally, the dancing elephant" by the ringmaster. His spiel included such illustrative terms as "Prancing, Playful Pachyderm"—the usual circus lingo. The spotlight then focused on Sally, draped in scarlet regalia. A rumba beat began. To the rhythm of the music, Sally would kick out one leg and then another as she slowly "danced" from the first ring to the second and the third and then finally offstage at the left.

But there was a problem. An intestinal problem.

Once she had initially displayed her unique ability to "dance" to the rumba beat, a large wad of green fecal matter spurted out her rear end. And then it happened the next time she kicked out her leg. It seemed to occur every time she kicked out a leg—on and on and on. When she got to the center ring, Sally stood on her head. Now the spurting wads of feces shot into the air repeatedly, like a fountain! When she once again stood and advanced to the third ring, it just kept coming. The poor clowns following the elephant with brooms had their work cut out for them.

The response from the audience was electrifying. Roars of laughter filled the Garden. Ahead of us sat a young couple. Initially they were doing a considerable amount of cuddling, but when Sally started putting on her display, the young man began laughing uncontrollably — so much so that he slipped out of his seat and lay on the floor, convulsing with laughter. His companion, however, wasn't amused.

While seated at the bar awaiting the bus, faculty members Tim Hunter and Gene Carter were regaled by my description of the goings on at the circus.

Then Tim, in a matter-of fact manner said, "You were lucky. You had fun. Not me. We spent the day roaming the city with Gene and Karen (Gene's wife). They have to be the most boring people I've ever spent time with."

All of this at a small table with the "boring" couple. I couldn't believe my ears!!

Booze problems

Alcoholic beverages were not allowed on the bus, so the students simply carried it in their stomachs. On one trip, a club member approached me in the morning as we were boarding the bus. "I have my 15-year-old brother with me, he said. He had the day off school and we couldn't find anyone to stay with him at home, so I thought I'd bring him along. Will that be OK, Mr. Stevens?"

"Welcome aboard!" I greeted the 15 -year-old. I was to regret it later on.

It wasn't long after boarding the bus at 11 p.m. that I became aware that the 15- year-old had been drinking. It soon became obvious to all of the riders when the boy hurled into the aisle, again and again. It was a disgusting sight, and the smell was even worse.

I felt responsible because I had extended permission for the young man to join us on the field trip. I found a bunch of paper towels in the lavatory of the bus and got down on my hands and knees, starting to clean up the mess. The more I thought about what I was doing, the more my stomach heaved. Regrettably, I then had two messes to clean up: the 15-year-old's and my own. It was the most miserable bus ride I have ever taken.

Mixers

They were called "mixers" in the '60s and '70s: beer parties put on by college students ostensibly to raise money to pay for club activities. They had to be held off-campus because alcohol was forbidden on-campus by college policy.

The Entrepreneurs weren't immune to fun. With considerable apprehension, I agreed to act as one of the chaperones for their mixer. Furthermore, I agreed to find a location for the event.

The first place I phoned was a popular watering hole/pavilion in a nearby town. "This is Mr. Stevens, advisor to Hudson College's Business Club. We'd like to schedule a mixer at your place."

"Where did you say you were from?" asked the prospective vendor.

"Hudson College," I reiterated.

There was a pause at the other end of the line. Then I got the news: "We will never again allow Hudson College students to have a party at our establishment," he said. "The last time you had a party here, there was a fight, and someone bit off the bartender's ear."

"I understand," I replied. Why wasn't I surprised?

We finally secured the local steamfitters union hall, and oh, what a night ensued. The entrance fee was $3 a person. All you could drink. No chips or pretzels, just beer, an endless supply of it. Two other faculty and I had agreed to serve as chaperones.

Unfortunately, I got caught up in the "fun", even though I was collecting and storing the cash in a cloth bag.

Harvard on the Hudson

There was a live band and a lot of dancing. What an experience. It went on until well after midnight.

The only mishap was when a disgruntled student staggered up to a female faculty member and said, "Hi, Mrs. Stone, remember me?" With that he proceeded to deliberately pour an entire pitcher of beer over her head.

It seems that the guilty student was a drop out. He had failed Mrs. Stone's accounting class as well as others and was about to be dismissed for academic reasons, so he quit. That was a year ago.

The student was apprehended by other students and forced to apologize as well as to pay in advance for cleaning Mrs. Stone's clothes.

I was really on edge about the whole matter, but it seemed to be settled without calling in the police. And I had to admit to myself that Mrs. Stone looked funny as hell with her hair dripping like a wet puppy.

I continued to enjoy the merriment right to the end.

I was really dismayed the following morning when I couldn't find any of the cash I'd collected—hundreds of dollars.

I phoned the Dean. "Adam, I can't find any of the cash I collected. I put it all in a cloth bag and now it's missing!"

There was no consolation from my boss, who responded, "Somewhere out there is a rich thief!" I was really upset.

Frantically I conducted a more thorough search of my bedroom. When I reached way into the back of my desk drawer, I clutched a handful of dollar bills. And there were more and more and more. What a relief! It was all there! Some sot had deliberately stuffed all of the money back in the drawer as far as he could reach. That certain sot was someone who at this moment was suffering from a very bad hangover!

From that experience I learned two lessons that I have carried through the rest of my life: (1) Be very wary of college-aged students when it comes to booze. They may legally be adults, but they can still be immature. (2) Never be the sole guardian of cash. In the future I would ask a dozen faculty members to help out as chaperones, and as the evening progressed, I would dole out no more than $50 of cash in a labeled envelope to each chaperone.

The final mixer took place at a brand new club in Albany, the Polish Community Center. It was a mistake never to be repeated. The mixers had become so popular that they had gotten out of hand. Young people who were complete strangers to the Business Department showed up to join in the fun. One anonymous drunk threw a beer can through the neon sign advertising the club. Another destroyed upholstery on some of the bar stools.

At that point I drew the line. The time had come to quit. Property destruction was simply not acceptable. The core of the Entrepreneurs was a fine group, but when outsiders were added, things got out of hand.

Harvard on the Hudson

After several years, the students lost interest in the Entrepreneurs club and it was disbanded. I was relieved. It had been fun while it lasted. However, enough is enough!

CHAPTER SEVEN—COLLEGE AUXILIARY PERSONNEL

Students, faculty, and administrative personnel constitute the main body of college employees. An additional cadre of employees is often overlooked, and they are the ones most vital to the institution. These are the secretaries, administrative assistants, custodians, security guards, maintenance, and other support staff who literally keep the college in operation. Those who are smart enough to recognize the support staff's valuable contribution to the life of the college make their own lives so much easier. And they also enjoy the fun of working with them.

Sarge

"Sarge" is a case in point. He'd been hired from a security firm to patrol the student parking lot and manage traffic. He operated mainly in the open air, and he had a booming voice that could not be ignored. When warm weather came, and it was necessary to have the classroom windows open, his thundering curse words would fill the air. Lectures would be temporarily halted simply to enjoy the string of oaths wafting in the summer air. "Get that (expletive) car out of this parking lot, you sneaky (expletive)!"

"I'll kick your (expletive) if I ever catch you in this area again!"

He wasn't only tough on the students. One day an elderly dignified female representative from the local phone company was scheduled to talk to a secretarial class. It wasn't surprising that she had trouble finding a place to park with the limited space available. So she parked in a space reserved for administrative personnel. It didn't take Sarge long to come upon the scene. He immediately began cursing the frustrated guest for parking in the wrong location. But this lady was sharp. "Since you know the campus better than I," she said politely, "perhaps you can find a more appropriate place to park." With that she deftly flipped her car keys into his hand. Sarge knew he had lost that round.

It wasn't long after that incident, that Sarge was relieved of his duties at the college. The last time I saw him, he was barking orders in a more subdued manner at the local airport.

Margaret Knows All

And then there was Margaret. She was somewhat hulky and a little mentally challenged, but she sure knew what was going on at the college. In the early years, the semester ran until mid-June, and that always posed a question about how Memorial Day would be handled in terms of a day off from classes.

One year, Memorial Day fell on a Saturday, and somehow the college calendar did not provide for the Friday classes to be canceled. This upset the students considerably. The president of the college was pressed for a decision, and he firmly stated that classes would not be canceled. A week before Memorial Day, Margaret stopped by my office, which at the time housed three other colleagues, and proceeded to dust my desk. Margaret always moved at snail's pace, preferring to dust around, rather than under, such items as books, phones, etc. She would very slowly go about her work. Stella VanAuken, head of the Secretarial department, and I were two of the four who shared the office, and we thoroughly enjoyed each other's company. We were smart enough to know Margaret's value as an insider.

"Margaret, what do you hear about the day before Memorial Day? I asked. "Will we have it off?"

"Yes we will, Mr. Stevens," Margaret responded.

I begged to differ, "I hear that the president has firmly stated that classes will be held."

After the president's initial decision, the students continued agitating for the day before Memorial Day to be a holiday. This time the president stood his ground even more firmly. There was to be no day off before Memorial Day.

When Margaret next came around to the office, I once again asked, "Margaret, what do you know about the status of the day before Memorial Day. To which she calmly answered, "We'll be having the day before Memorial Day off."

Boy is she wrong I thought to myself and I said, "I don't think you are right, Margaret. The students have been agitating, and they have the president's dander up. I'm sure we won't be getting the day off."

A day later, there was a full-fledged student demonstration. The president directly engaged them and most authoritatively announced that classes would not be canceled the day before Memorial Day.

The next day, Margaret reappeared. Since the last word had been given and the decision made at the highest level, I warily approached Margaret on the subject once again. "Margaret, what do you know about the day before Memorial Day?" I inquired.

Margaret's response: "Mr. Stevens, we're gonna' have the day before Memorial Day off."

And guess what? We had the day before Memorial Day off. The lesson: never underestimate support staff.

George Geneva—Food Service Director

George Geneva came onto the scene to manage the college cafeteria not long after the new campus opened. He had his work cut out for him. As mentioned earlier, President Otto was a tyrant—and a cheap one at that. George survived by befriending him and successive college presidents as well. His job got more and more complicated as the college enrollment expanded.

After thirty some years of service, George retired. In his retirement speech, George made a most startling confession: "You all should know that in all of my years as manager of the cafeteria, I never made any decaffeinated coffee. None! Oh yes, I had a lot of orange coffee container covers, but I never made decaffeinated coffee!"

The audience at first did not respond, and then it erupted in applause accompanied by laughter.

Harriet

The cleaning woman, Harriet, was one fun person. She did her job but with no great enthusiasm. Often, she would be located in a darkened office taking a nap. But we couldn't help but love her. She was a cunning conniver. Hal Hampton, a teaching colleague, and Harriet thoroughly enjoyed each other. One afternoon, Harriet was cleaning the hallway baseboards—in a fashion. Hal saw her wasting time at the task, and he told her that she was going about the job all wrong, that more effort was needed in the scrubbing process. "What are you saying?" Harriet asked. "Are you trying to tell me that I don't know how to do my job, Mr. Hampton?"

"Here, let me show you what you should be doing," Hal responded, getting down on his hands and knees and taking the steel wool cleaning pad from her hands. He proceeded to vigorously scrub the baseboard clean as Harriett stood by in amused contemplation. "Mr. Hampton, why don't you just continue along the baseboard until you reach the end of the hallway," she joked. To those of us who knew Harriet, this was a most hilarious illustration of her cunningness.

Elmond Merton, the Custodian

Before coming to work as a custodian at the college, Elmond Merton was a local dairy farmer, just barely scraping out an existence. He hired on so that he could be covered by hospitalization and build up a pension. Like so many farmers, Elmond was a practical, down-to-earth guy who had a multitude of capabilities. He was also fun to be with, spinning yarns about his years on the farm, etc.

There are some who treat custodians as menial assistants because they do not have faculty status. What a mistake! A wealth of useful knowledge can be gained from support staff, and do some of them know the dirt—the juicy goings on that no one would suspect.

The head of the custodian department and the college switchboard operator, both of whom were married (but not to each other) were having a daily tryst. Elmond discovered them early one morning when he overheard moans and groans emanating from the janitors' boot closet.

Since Elmond and this boss were not very fond of each other for a number of reasons the farmer slyly let the information slip off his tongue.

I had always been curious as to why the switchboard operator would be coming toward my classroom building in the early morning hours before classes were in session. She was so anxious for the tryst that often her headphones were dangling from her ears as she crossed the campus.

The Harried Switchboard Operator

By the early '80s, the college was bursting at the seams. There were never enough parking spaces for the students and the faculty. Classrooms were constantly being rescheduled to accommodate the hordes of students, and the antiquated switchboard was constantly jammed.

Harvard on the Hudson

One early autumn morning when classes hadn't yet started, I noticed that I was not getting any telephone calls from off campus. That was unusual, because the phone had been constantly ringing in previous semesters.

The switchboard was overtaxed. It hadn't been updated for a decade or so, and the operator (when not having her tryst) was simply overwhelmed.

In the late afternoon, I would get calls from parents who were furious with the college because their earlier calls did not get through. One parent lamented, "I let that phone ring 23 times, and no one answered. What is going on in that place?"

I received several calls with similar complaints. Finally, it was time to take action.

First, before doing anything at all, I carefully considered my approach to the problem. Should I call the switchboard operator's supervisor, or should I talk to the operator myself? Rather than get her in trouble with her boss, I opted to discuss the problem with the source.

"Carolyn," I said, using my most tactful tone of voice, "Is there a problem with the switchboard? I don't seem to be getting many calls early in the day, and I am receiving complaints from parents trying to get in touch with me."

Her response was totally unexpected. Carolyn savagely snarled into the phone, "Oh, yeah? You think there's a problem, do you? Why don't you come over here and try doing my job: plugging wires in and out of sockets, listening to people bitching and moaning, losing incoming calls. It's no picnic, and I don't appreciate you reminding me of it!" With that, Carolyn slammed down the phone.

"So much for diplomacy," I concluded. My next call was to Carolyn's supervisor. Not only was there a switchboard problem, but there was an attitude problem as well.

The Protective Secretary

One time I had made a luncheon appointment with a long-time chairperson colleague, Austra Meurs. We were scheduled to meet at noon, but something came up, and I knew I would have to delay for perhaps as long as an hour. It was most important to contact Austra. I phoned her office, and her secretary answered. I had no idea that the lady was so "inclined" to be protective of her boss.

"Is Austra available?" I asked.

"She isn't in. She's at home," the secretary curtly responded.

"May I have her home phone number?"

"No you cannot! I have strict instructions never to give out her home number," she declared.

"But we have an appointment shortly that I have to change. We've been close friends for years. Won't you please give me her phone number?"

"No, I will not," she snapped. More curtness.

"Look, I don't think you understand the situation. We have a luncheon appointment scheduled at noon, and I have to tell her I can't make it at that time. Please give me her home phone number."

"Absolutely not!" she responded.

My next option was to pull rank. "I'm not sure you know who I am," I stated authoritatively. This is Mr. Stevens, chairperson of the Accounting Department. It's most important that I speak with Austra Meurs."

"I DON'T CARE IF YOU'RE JOHN PAUL JONES!" she said. "You're not getting her number."

With that, I hung up the phone and had a good, frustrated laugh. Somehow the luncheon situation got resolved, but I vowed never again to get entangled with that loyal secretary.

CHAPTER EIGHT—MEMORABLE SHENANIGANS AND OTHER GOINGS ON

So many isolated instances during my 43-year tenure at Hudson College have become indelible memories.

The Valentine Gift

My wife, Sandy, was one in a million. She was a wonderful wife, an excellent mother to our seven offspring, and a great caregiver—qualities that endeared her to all who came in contact with her. She was an attractive blonde with a sunny disposition. And she was reserved, most of the time. But there were times when she would step out of character, like the time she appeared at the college on Valentine's Day.

Sandy had called the Business Division secretary in advance to find out when and where I was in class. It so happened that I was teaching a Statistics class across the hall from the Dean's office when there came a knock on the door. There stood Sandy. I couldn't have been more surprised.

"Happy Valentine's Day!" she said in a loud voice so that my entire class could hear. "I've brought you a card and a gift, which I want you to open in front of the students."

I was bewildered. This was so out of character for Sandy.

She handed me a card and said, "Open it and read it in front of the students."

I did as instructed. The card read, "For our next get-away weekend together."

Then she told me to open the gift.

Removing the wrapping paper revealed a white cardboard box about a foot long, and three inches thick.

When I opened the box, I found it contained a whip and chains, which I dutifully held up for all to see.

The class went into an uproar as they pictured their sixtyish-year-old teacher heading for a weekend of debauchery!

Needless to say, I knew there was nothing more that could be done with that class, and so I dismissed them promptly.

The Teddy Bear

Sandy and I had presented our first grandchild with a black teddy bear for her second birthday. It wasn't just any teddy bear. It was huge—reaching about five feet tall and in a permanent sitting position.

Surely it was a gift she would never forget.

The gift was overruled by the maternal grandmother, who declared that the bear was much too scary for a two-year-old. My wife and I reluctantly agreed and cordially accepted the return of this giant, menacing-looking toy animal.

What to do with a huge black teddy bear? Naturally, I took it to the college. Surely there was fun to be had with such a prize!

The first prank required collusion between me and my friend Stella, head of the Secretarial Department.

My office just happened to be one floor above that of another colleague, Don Gilmart, head of the Criminal Justice Department. For some reason, Don always kept his window blinds down, probably to fend off the glare of the afternoon sun. I pondered how to unnerve unflappable Don. I came upon the solution: lower the huge bear out of my own office window by tying a cord around the bear's neck and then feeding out the cord until the hulking black creature was at the desk level of Don's shuttered window.

But how to get Don's attention, since he couldn't see out the window?

That's where Stella came in. When I had completed lowering the bear to just the right level, Stella phoned Don. When he answered the phone, she said, "Don, open your window blind. There's been an accident out on the highway that you really should see."

With that, Don opened the blind and was completely taken aback by the huge toy bear peering into his window. "Holy f——!" he shouted, so loudly that it could be heard throughout the corridors.

With that success under my belt, I was determined to have even more fun using the black bear.

By this time it was late in the day, and another teaching colleague of mine, Roger Champion, was teaching a late-afternoon Statistics class just down the hall from my office. (It should be mentioned here that Roger was a very principled, respected faculty member who was in so many ways a "nice guy." Very religious. Very professional. Very much of a role model for the students.)

I stealthily carried the monstrous black toy down the hall, and when I came close to Roger's class, I sat the bear down and then quietly pushed it until it sat directly in front of the classroom door. All this time, Roger was lecturing the class, looking directly at them and intently imparting the subject matter of the day.

Then Roger paused from his presentation and turned his head toward the corridor. The shocked result was perfect—in my opinion. Roger loudly exclaimed, "Holy s— -!" —something he would never do in front of a class in a million years!

The students, of course, were delighted, and they roared when they heard the exclamation and found out what had caused it.

There were interesting aftermaths to the teddy-bear incident.

Roger was furious with me. He resented that the shocking intrusion had caused him to lose his cool in front of the class. I apologized for my indiscretion.

A very different reaction came from the college President, who phoned me some time later.

"I happened to be driving onto the campus not too long ago, when I looked toward your building and saw what I first thought to be King Kong climbing up the outside wall. What was that all about?" he asked. He thoroughly enjoyed hearing about the details involved in the harmless pranks.

Harvard on the Hudson

Coding Students

There were so many routines and similar student situations over the years that on one occasion, I had the brainstorm of using coding when communicating with other chairpersons. For example, literally dozens of students with low ability mathematical skills (as proved by course grades) became academically hopeless in my accounting program and henceforth aspired to become—of all things—computer experts. They may have had academic talent in other areas, but not in the math that would be required in computer programming.

Consequently, many of my advisees would stop by my office to see what was required to transfer from the Accounting Department to the Computer Studies Department. "The first step is to set up an interview with the Chairman of the Computer Studies Department," I would tell them. Then I got the idea to alert the other chairman that a student was hopelessly unqualified to make the transfer. So I would give the potential transferring student a note to show to the chair of the Computer Department.

The first time this happened, I received a phone call from the Computer Department colleague. "This student just came into my office," he said. "She said she wanted to make a transfer from your department to mine and handed me this note. It reads "DKD." What is that all about?"

It means she "Doesn't Know Dickshit," I responded. "She is hopeless in math."

The Tire-Tread Incident

One wintertime, I was having car trouble, not an unusual problem. I borrowed my brother's dilapidated pickup truck to get to and from classes until my car was fixed. Along with a multitude of other problems, the floor on the passenger's side of the truck cabin had rotted out to the extent that the highway could clearly be seen by looking down through the floor on the passenger side of the vehicle.

I had gathered up a batch of accounting test papers and had decided to take them home for grading. To me, it was always important to get the results back to the students as soon as time permitted.

It was a rainy day, and the road was slushy. At one intersection I made a quick stab at the brakes when I saw a stop light ahead. At least the damned truck had good brakes! With the sudden stop, the unpackaged pile of tests on the passenger seat slipped off the seat and cascaded down through the gaping hole in the floor and onto the road below. I pulled over but too late to prevent the rear wheel from running over the scattered test papers.

What to do? I decided to ignore the problem and grade the papers, nevertheless.

Harvard on the Hudson

The next day, I handed back the graded papers to the eagerly awaiting class. There was a pause of a minute or so, and then the reactions started.

"Mr. Stevens, there are tire-tread marks on my paper. It looks like a Firestone to me. What happened?" A ripple of laughter broke out from others whose papers were marked by tire treads.

It took some time to quell the reactions and get the class back to order.

The Unfortunate Hitchhiker

For years, I drove my 1931 Model A Ford roadster to the college — even during the winter. I had fashioned Plexiglas side windows, which cut down on the howling wind but had little effect on the heat inside the car.

One day while driving to the college, I saw one of my students hitchhiking at the side of the road. I stopped and welcomed the boy to join me for the rest of the ride to Hudson College. I was anxious to see the student's reaction to riding in the Model A as it chugged onward.

The student, Charles Summers, sat silently with his teeth chattering. Then he asked, "Mr. Stevens, doesn't the cold bother you?"

I decided to respond philosophically. "Mr. Summers, (adhering to my policy of addressing my students by their last name) cold is a relative thing, don't you think? For instance, if we were in Alaska, one would probably think it was rather warm, wouldn't you agree?"

Charles Summers just shook his head in disbelief. He couldn't wait to get out of the car and into a warm classroom.

An Evening with Henny Youngman

The college assessed students for a Student Activity Fee. The money collected was managed by the students and was used to pay for guest speakers, performers, etc., to come onto the campus. On one occasion, they chose veteran comedian Henny Youngman.

To me it seemed incongruous for college-aged students to bring in a 78-year-old Borscht Belt comic, even though the man had an international reputation for delivering his "one liners," — brief hilarious jokes.

This was a rare opportunity not to be missed so I invited my wife and several family members to attend the evening performance.

Henny stepped out on the stage, accompanied by his base violin, his prop. He seated himself on a chair, and his first comment was, "Is there a piano player in the house? I need to be accompanied by a piano player."

I felt nudges and eventually I stood up and volunteered to undertake the piano playing assignment. I'd always played by ear, not requiring music sheets. My experience was limited to family occasions, and I was reluctant to get up in front of an audience. On the other hand, I thoroughly enjoyed Henny Youngman, and Henny needed assistance.

Up onto the stage I went, striding over to the console piano and taking a seat at the keyboard. A round of spattered applause accompanied my actions.

Henny said, "Play something—anything—just so I can tell if you're any good." So I started to play something simple and familiar.

Henny broke in, "Can I ask you a question? When did you break your fingers?" The audience roared. Me too!

Again a comment from Henny after I resumed playing, "I think we've found the lost chord!" More laughter from the audience, and by this time I was laughing so much that I damned near fell off the piano stool. It was obvious that I was just another prop for the guy.

Then came a volley of jokes from the seasoned entertainer.

"I said to my mother-in-law when she came for a visit: my house is your house. So she sold it!"

"A grandmother in Miami takes her two-year-old grandson to the beach. A huge wave comes up and sweeps him out to sea. She is devastated. But along come the Coast Guard, the police, the firemen, and the lifeguard. They find the youngster, bring him back onto the beach, give him CPR, and bring him back to life." The grandmother says to the rescuers, "He had a hat!"

"A guy goes into a bar and the bartender says to him, 'Will you do me a favor?' 'Sure,' answers the newcomer. 'Will you please take this guy at the bar home?' says the bartender. 'He's too drunk to drive.' So the guy doing the favor puts his arm around the drunk and helps him out of the barroom. When he gets to the door, he leans the drunk against the wall, and the drunk falls down. So he picks him up, opens the door, and hauls him out to his car. He leans the guy against the car so he can open the door and the guy falls down. He picks up the guy, puts him in the passenger side of his car, and finds the guy's wallet to get his address. He drives the guy to his home, gets out of the car, hauls out the drunk, stands him against the car, and the drunk falls down. So he lugs him to his home doorway and rings the bell. In order to do this, he props the guy up in the doorway and the guy falls down. Just then, the door opens and out steps this little old lady, the drunk guy's mother. 'Thanks for bringing him home,' she says, 'but where is his wheelchair?'"

On and on went the hilarious anecdotes. Henny spieled them out from memory.

"I said to my wife, 'What do you want for our 25th anniversary?' She says, 'Take me somewhere I've never been before.' So I took her into the kitchen!"

It was a fun-filled evening, never to be forgotten. And the best part was playing the foil for the old guy while admiring his stamina.

Impersonating a Man of the Cloth

How to be in two different places at the same time? That was the dilemma facing me, and it required some degree of ingenuity.

A colleague at the college had undergone a hysterectomy a few days earlier. She was recuperating at the Albany Medical Center. At the same time, my son Greg was in nearby St. Peter's Hospital on the mend from a broken leg. My work schedule didn't permit much extra time, so I attempted to visit both patients during the very narrow visiting-hour time frames of each hospital.

It was a challenge.

"Those visiting hours rules can't possibly apply to the clergy," I reasoned in an unusual burst of resourcefulness. "Let me see — I have this large, black-covered accounting textbook that just might pass for a Bible. My straw boater hat and dark suit with white shirt and black tie should promote an austere image. Add to the mix a white collar fashioned from adding machine tape and *voila!* the appearance of being clergyman. Brilliant! No harm in trying!

I left my office with the book in hand, put the machine tape in place, and placed the straw hat jauntily on my head. Within a half hour I was entering the parking lot of the Albany Medical Center.

"Well, I made it this far successfully," I thought. "Now to see if my ruse will allow me to visit Joan Browne outside of visiting hours. Then I can drive up to St. Peter's to spend a little time with Greg."

The parking lot attendant at the Medical Center suspiciously eyed the car. He strolled over and announced, "The parking fee is $2."

"You charge the clergy for parking?" I inquired with caution.

The young man blushed. "I'm sorry, sir, I didn't notice your collar. You are right; there's no charge for clergy. Go right in and stay as long as you need to."

"It worked!" I inwardly rejoiced.

The next stop was at the visitor's desk to find Joan's room number. Without raising her eyes to see me, the volunteer at the desk said, "Visiting hours do not begin until a half hour from now."

When she looked up, she did a double take, peering over her half-rimmed glasses at the dignified looking gentleman with the dark suit and collar and carrying a black book. "I'm so sorry, Father. Whom did you wish to visit? Joan Browne? She's in C317 at the end of the hall. Take a right and you'll see the elevators. Go right up!"

"Passed another hurdle," I chuckled to myself.

There was an unexpected setback, however, when I stepped quietly into Joan's room. It was dark and the blinds were drawn. Joan was dozing, gradually gaining strength after her surgical ordeal.

She became aware of a visitor and awoke with a start. Seeing the dark figure in the doorway, she assumed it was a priest. Feeling as poorly as she did, she assumed I was there to administer last rites. Then she recognized me.

"You asshole. You scared the daylights out of me," Joan chided, breathing a sigh of relief. "Sit down next to the bed. Let's have a good chat. How's everything going back at the college?"

She scowled at me. "What in hell are you wearing?" she asked.

"Shh! I'm posing as a man of the cloth to get around this place's rigid visiting- hours schedule. I have to get up to St. Peter's and then back to the college before too much time passes."

We had a great visit. After that, I jauntily made it across the parking lot to my car. For some reason, however, my knees grew weak as I thought about the complications that could have arisen out of my deceptive prank. "Just suppose some other patient was dying and someone saw me in the hall and asked me to perform last rites? I asked myself. "I never thought of that...wow!"

Once I'd left the parking lot, my confidence returned. The black book and the collar would no longer be needed. I would be in time to visit son Greg during scheduled visiting hours at St. Peters. That visit, too, went well, and I got back to the college with time to spare.

Heady with the success of a good adventure, I couldn't wait to share my experience with my sister, Jane, who was an Elder in a small Presbyterian church. I phoned her that evening. She thought my impersonation was hilarious! Later in the week, she attended her church where her minister was Dr. Carlyle Adams. He was an ecclesiastical expert and a renowned theologian. He prided himself on his knowledge of clerical clothing, including collars.

Following Sunday service, Dr. Adams, who knew me quite well, approached Jane with a twinkle in his eye. "You know, I thought I knew all there is to know about clerical attire, but this week I saw a clergyman at the Medical Center wearing a collar I simply couldn't identify. I can't for the life of me think of the religious sect he belonged to. Would you have any idea, Jane?" he inquired with a knowing smile.

Harvard on the Hudson

The Visit to a Motor Vehicle Office

All the time during which I was teaching at Hudson College, I'd seldom had a pleasant experience when dealing with the Motor Vehicle Department. It had gotten so that I dreaded the harassment by clerks who seemed more interested in giving the customer a hard time than getting vehicles registered.

During those years of raising seven children and living on a mediocre salary, I couldn't afford decent transportation. I would pay a few hundred dollars for a clunker that would last maybe two years or so. This time around, I had acquired a used station wagon from a woman in West Albany, some twenty miles away. At the time of the transaction, the woman had made a minor mistake when signing the document. She made an erasure and then she wrote in the corrected signature. I thought little of it at the time, but that minor error was to become a nightmare.

I had some free time at noon, and I told my secretary I would be leaving the campus but should be returning within an hour or so.

Off I drove to the Motor Vehicle Office in Troy to register my clunker.

The waiting line was short, and in no time I was presenting the clerk with what I thought was a complete and acceptable packet of papers.

Alice, the clerk, studied the transfer papers and then made the dreaded statement: "Uh Oh." When I inquired as to the nature of the problem, Alice (with that 'gotcha' look in her eye) replied, "There seems to be an erasure made on the signature line."

I knew about the erasure but was sure it wouldn't be a problem. "It isn't so serious a problem that it will hold me up is it? I asked. "I have to get back to the college because I have a class to teach." I was sure that would win her over.

Alice was not to be persuaded and stood her ground. "You'll just have to go back to the owner and get a replacement form signed, sir."

I was becoming exasperated. "May I please talk to your supervisor?" I politely asked. Little did I know that Alice and the supervisor, Martha, were the closest of friends.

"Martha, what do you think? Is there or is there not an obvious erasure on this form?" Martha would agree to anything her buddy said. And she did just that.

I was defeated. I picked up a replacement blank form and went to the phone to contact the seller. I was in luck. She was still at home. I drove to her house, got the form signed, and headed back toward Troy.

That's when it occurred to me that the Motor Vehicle Office in Albany was closer, so I chose to get the car registered there. I presented the Albany clerk with the papers. While reading over the documents, the young man uttered the dreaded "Uh Oh!" I shuddered. The guillotine was once more about to fall.

"What's the problem?" I asked.

"One of these forms says your car is a 1961 Plymouth station wagon, but someone in your insurance company typed in the year 1960. You will have to get a replacement form from your insurance company."

"But the insurance company is twenty miles away from here and I'll never make it to the college in time for class. Can't you just put that insurance form in your typewriter and change that 0 to a 1?" I may just as well have asked the guy to commit murder. He refused to make the correction, and I was directed back to my insurance office.

The young man added: "Be sure to take along this new insurance form."

I looked at the new form and noticed it was yellow. The one I had gotten from the insurance company was white. "Don't worry about the difference in colors," the young guy assured me. "We use a yellow form in Albany, but it is just as acceptable as the white one," Warily, I took the form and drove back to the insurance company to get the change made. By this time more than two hours had passed since I left the office.

From the insurance company, I decided to return to the Motor Vehicle Office in Troy because it was much closer to the college.

Sure enough, when I got to the front of the line, I was once again facing the severe stare of Alice, the original executioner. I was literally trembling when I handed the revised papers over to Alice.

She was reading the papers when she uttered that horrible phrase, "Uh Oh."

I meekly asked, "What's the matter this time?"

"This insurance form is yellow. The one we use in this office is white."

I knew I was trapped. I felt betrayed because the clerk in Albany had guaranteed that the yellow form would be acceptable.

"Isn't there something you can do to help me out? My class comes up in less than a half hour, and I just don't have time to spend running around to correct minor problems. Please let me get back to the college!" I begged.

Alice called Martha over, explaining the new problem with the different colored form.

"Shall we let him go?" she asked her supervisor. Martha winked at Alice and Alice winked at me. "You're fine.

You're free to go on your way. We'll accept the yellow form."

Heaving a sigh of relief, I returned to the campus, just in time to cover my class.

The Embarrassing Lavatory Intrusion

In the 1960s and '70s, the campus grew phenomenally. It was a constant source of frustration trying to find important documents because they would be moved from one location to another as the campus developed and new buildings appeared. When I first started teaching at the college, there were just four buildings. Otto Gunstrom, its first president, had his office in the same building where I had my office and where most of my classes were held. Later, Gunstrom's office was moved to a building that had once been a one-story private home.

Miriam, the president's secretary, a divorcee in her 50s, was a joy to work with because of her competence and her sense of humor. Over the years, she and I grew to be close friends who thoroughly enjoyed each other's company.

At the end of the academic year, boxes of diplomas were customarily picked up and carried back to their offices by the academic chairpersons. For some reason or other, there was always confusion as to where the diploma covers were stored.

Since there were so many students getting their diplomas on graduation day, the college mercifully tailored the graduation ceremony to be as brief as possible. One short cut was that each department as a unit was introduced in lieu of reading off the name of each graduate before he or she crossed the stage to receive a diploma and shake hands with the president and other college officials. The students as a department rose and mounted the steps to walk across the stage. Instead of stretching out the ceremony for hours, it was all over within forty-five minutes.

To make sure that students did not get the wrong personalized degree, they were given only a dark-green diploma cover containing a note telling them to report to the chairperson's office to pick up the degree itself. I enjoyed this tradition, because it gave me the opportunity to personally congratulate my department's graduates before they left campus for the final time.

The physical collection of the degrees by the chairpersons is another story. One year in the 70s, I volunteered to get the degrees for both myself and my office mate, the head of the Secretarial Department. I was told that they were to be picked up in the building where the president's office was located.

Since the president's office had recently been moved, to a different building, I had no idea which room contained the diplomas. I'd had never been in the place before. Miriam was not at her desk when I arrived, so I took a guess as to which door led to the room where the diplomas were stored. When I opened the door, I was greeted by a shriek. There sat Miriam on the toilet seat! Both Miriam and I were shocked and embarrassed. When she recovered somewhat, she ordered me to get out and to shut the door behind me.

I was directed to the proper room where the diplomas were stored. As I was leaving the building with my arms laden with boxes, I overheard Miriam on the telephone with a colleague: "It was bad enough to be caught on the toilet seat, but it had to be Bill Stevens. Now the whole campus will know how he found me on the john!"

I assured Miriam that the matter was between her and me and that regarding the incident, my lips were sealed.

I didn't say for how long!

When I got back to my office, I couldn't wait to impart the incident to my Secretarial Department chair colleague who always thoroughly enjoyed a good story. In the late afternoon, a campus-wide meeting of chairpersons was scheduled to be held. Stella, my fun Secretarial Department colleague, accompanied me to the meeting. When we arrived, there stood Miriam, greeting the arriving attendants. When she saw me, her face flushed. Stella blurted out, "Oh, Miriam, I thought it was a riot about Bill catching you on the toilet seat."

Talk about getting a withering glare! Miriam's laser look just about melted me on the spot!

CHAPTER NINE—-AUSTRALIAN INTERLUDE

The Adventure with its Ensuing Adjustments

I had married Sandy in 1957. There followed high school and college teaching, and also children. For many, this would be enough of a fulfilling career. Not for me, however. I had long nurtured a yearning to get away from the routine. In 1964, at the age of 32 and after talking it over with Sandy, I decided to try teaching for a year in Australia. I chose that country because the language would be familiar and the climate enjoyable. Also, that country had so much allure in terms of a free- spirited citizenry, awesome scenery and the reputed Aussies friendship toward Americans. In World War II, the USA had been their salvation after attacks by the Japanese forces, and they were still mindful of that.

Finding a job wasn't easy. I decided to contact the New York State Commissioner of Education, a man who might have some knowledge of overseas teaching opportunities.

Sure enough, my home phone rang one winter morning in 1965. "This is the Commissioner's secretary," announced the voice at the other end of the line. "We are expecting an educator from Australia this afternoon and are wondering if you would like to meet him."

I was flabbergasted. Of course I would be there.

The outcome was a suggestion from the Australian educator that I apply to the Royal Melbourne Institute of Technology (RMIT), a 25,000 student college in downtown Melbourne, Victoria, Australia. The Australian visitor warned that high school teaching in Australia would have limited appeal to me because of the low salaries.

I wrote to the director of the School of Business at RMIT. In April, I received the invitation to teach at a salary of 1,800 pounds, the equivalent of $3,600 a year. Having studied the standard of living in Australia, I judged that it was doable. I accepted the offer. The job was to begin in July, which necessitated a flurry of activity: notification to the community college, booking air flights, packing up a family of six, and bidding adieu for one year to other family and friends. Somehow it all came together.

Initially the Australian experience involved considerable adjustments. For one thing, July was mid-winter in Melbourne. Temperatures often hovered in the low 50's and it rained frequently. Few homes had central heat. For some reason, a promising housing deal had fallen through, and my family and I found ourselves living in an urban boarding house with one kitchen and one bathroom to serve about a dozen residents. It was a miserable situation. Vowing to get better accommodations, I bought a newspaper and found an ad for a suburban rental. I located the place by bus, and thereafter made a contract with the rental agent. With the help of a thoughtful boarding house owner, my wife and four children and I were packed into a car, driven out to East Doncaster, and deposited at our rental home.

For the first few months it was hard going. I had no car, which meant a lengthy walk to the nearest bus stop. I would ride the bus a few miles and then transfer to a trolley car for the final leg of the journey to RMIT. Sandy and I had left behind a large and closely-knit extended family, and now we found ourselves isolated on the outskirts of Melbourne. We were very lonesome.

Our first friends were the family of a carpenter named Bud who had emigrated from Minnesota. Bud was told by the local postmaster that "a family of Yanks had moved into the area." Bud wasted no time in contacting me. He had come to Australia under similar circumstances, with a wife and small children. He knew what it was to be lonely and was determined to ease the isolation pain for Sandy and me and our small children. Bud and his wife extended invitations to dinner and for visits. They were particularly thoughtful at Christmas. All during this time, I was gradually getting to know the Aussie faculty at the college.

By October, friendships with teaching colleagues began to gel. Enjoying a beer or two or three on Friday afternoons promoted close relationships. I began bringing home my teaching colleagues, first as individuals and later in couples. At last Sandy had some adult companionship. By this time, it became obvious that our brief stopover in Hawaii on the way to Melbourne had produced lasting results — Sandy was pregnant with offspring #5!

As summer approached, the weather improved. By this time, we had befriended several faculty and their families, and we began receiving social invitations as a couple and sometimes even as our entire family. Since no one at the college was paid very well, gatherings were modest in cost, but this in no way deterred budding relationships.

Infant Heather arrived in March. The social whirl had accelerated but had to be curtailed until the new arrival had matured enough to be taken thither and yon.

By the time the Stevens family departed in June, relationships with Australian friends had cemented to the extent that the farewell party was a tearful event.

Memorable Australian Experiences

<u>Acquiring a car:</u>

I relied upon public transportation for several weeks after arrival in Melbourne. Grocery shopping was an interesting experience, but the one-mile walk each way to and from the stores was exhausting. To complicate matters, there were no supermarkets back then. For veggies and fruits, one went to the green grocer, for meat to the butcher shop, for bread to the bakeshop, and for milk products to the dairy bar.

I needed a car, and the opportunity finally presented itself. An RMIT colleague, who eventually became my closest Aussie friend, told me that his aging father-in-law was ready to give up driving and wondered if I might be interested in the old guy's early '40s Wolseley, a British-made car with a solid reputation. I jumped at the chance.

Allen Holmes, my Aussie colleague, drove me to his father-in-law's house to see the car. It was old but in good condition, and it could accommodate my entire brood with a bit of a squeeze. When the old man showed me the boot (trunk), I spotted an American flag—wrapped around an oily jack.

"So much for the Australian love of Americans," I thought to myself.

The driving lesson was a whirlwind experience. Allen had other things to do, and he apparently assumed I was a quick study. How could that be? I had never before driven on the left-hand side of the road behind a steering wheel on the opposite side of the vehicle.

It was unnerving to have this guy mumbling directions in his particularly thick Aussie accent as I navigated the car down busy Melbourne streets. In a matter of minutes, I was deposited at curbside with this final statement from Allen. "You'll be right — no worries" as he casually flipped the keys into my hand. The drive back to East Doncaster was a terrifying experience for me. But at last I had a car!

Further Adjustments

Sons Grant and Mark had to be registered at the local elementary school, which was just a short walk from our rented house.

Homework assignments immediately arrived, and we thought they were mighty challenging. Right off the bat, the boys had an extensive list of spelling assignments to be practiced. It was a formidable task, and Sandy and I wasted no time in getting the boys to work. What an exhausting experience. Practice – tears — more practice — more tears.

By the end of the first week, the work was completed. That's when Sandy learned from the teacher that the assignment we had thought was due in one week wasn't due for a month!

East Doncaster was on the remote outskirts of Melbourne. Houses were spaced well apart, and there were children the same age as Mark and Grant in the neighboring homes. Someone thought it would be nice for the family to have a cat, and a grey kitten seemingly arrived out of nowhere. Dusty he was named.

Son Grant took a proprietary interest in the cat. In his very early years, Grant talked with a lisp, and one day Sandy overheard him exert his authority while showing the neighborhood children the newly arrived kitten. "Justht remember," Grant warned, "I'm that catsth bossth!"

Wintertime in Melbourne is challenging. Rarely is there snow, but nighttime temperatures often dip so low that ice forms inside of the windows, particularly because the house had no central heating. At first I thought to tackle the problem the old-fashioned way, by wielding an axe on the felled gum (eucalyptus) tree in our yard. It was a brutal experience. Gum tree wood is extremely dense and almost impossible to split.

At the time, most Aussies used soft coal briquettes in the fireplace and Melbourne residents were just beginning to change over to central heating using natural gas. Not us. We kept piling on more clothing to stave off the shivering. Once again, Bud Johnson came to the rescue, this time with a kerosene (paraffin in Aussie talk) stove. The smell of the burning fuel was awful, but the heat was most welcome.

At work in the faculty area, the offices were uncomfortably chilly. When commenting on the disagreeable temperatures to my boss and good friend, Allen, he retorted, "You Yanks are soft. You just can't take the cold. We Aussies are used to it and have no problems.

That's when I noticed that Allen had an electric heater under his desk. Soft indeed!

Beautiful Melbourne

For some years, polls have placed Melbourne in the top three of the most desirable cities in the world in which to live, ranking just behind Vancouver, Canada, and Vienna, Austria. If tree-filled parks are one of the criteria, it is easy to understand why Melbourne has such a high ranking.

I had first come to Melbourne in 1965. We made another visit in 1978 and again in 1996 and 2005 and 2010. The lasting friendships and the beauty of the city and surrounding areas were the main attractions. As the decades have passed, the city has grown ever more beautiful.

I loved strolling through the Botanical Gardens. With so much light rain in the winter and spring, all vegetation flourished. A walk through the park on a lunch break was an amazing treat. Other parks were nearly as beautiful. In recent years, the downtown Yarra River area has been enhanced by planned upgrading of the river area, even though the "beautiful blue Yarra" (like the Danube) is usually a murky brown.

The flowers throughout the area were dazzling. Such beautiful roses. Geraniums that grew six feet tall. In particular, I was dazzled by the colorful variety of cineraria in the park around the downtown Exhibition Building.

Harvard on the Hudson

Frequent dismal rains required another adjustment. Sandy and I had heard the Aussie banter on the train from Sydney to Melbourne. There is a traditional rivalry between the two major metropolises. Nothing serious, but fun to witness. Two older ladies were sniping. One said, "All you do in Sydney is lie around on the beach and worry about the sharks." Her rival retorted, "At least we have sunlight to enjoy. In Melbourne, it's nothing but constant rain."

I perked up at the shark reference, and I asked one of them how dangerous it was to swim in the ocean.

"Oh, it's really nothing," she replied. "They only get about six or seven of us in Australia each year." I was not reassured, since my family numbered six.

Transportation to downtown from home involved riding on electric trolley cars. The conductors, often cranky females, had a reputation for being abrupt with passengers. I recall counting out the fare in pennies, handing them all to the conductor, and then watching her cast the pennies into the street. She was too annoyed to bother with this Yank and his miserable change.

One faculty member, Tom Haines, constantly blamed the trams for being habitually late. "Bloody trams!" he cursed ever so repeatedly.

Australian food

Adjusting to the Australian diet was challenging. When I first bought a can of spaghetti at a grocery store, it was in a green sauce, and it was tasteless. Within a few years after we had returned to America, Melbourne evolved into a very cosmopolitan city, where the influx of Italians, Greeks, and Asians brought in culinary delights.

Shopping at the Victoria Market in the heart of Melbourne was a real adventure. I would drive to work on Fridays and would stock up on fresh meats, fruits, and veggies. The Market was a bustling area open only on Friday and Saturday. It occupied several city blocks and was located handily close to RMIT. Wise shoppers would stroll among the stalls with a list, writing down prices because the variation from one vendor to another could be considerable. Bananas could be ten cents a pound at one booth and twice that at another, without much difference in quality.

In later years, there was a movement by some municipal authorities to close the market. There ensued such an uproar that the plan was abandoned.

One memorable experience was with oranges. Never had I seen oranges so cheap, so I brought home dozens and dozens, which our family guzzled with ecstasy. No wonder I eventually broke out in a rash. The citric acid had done its work, causing me to scratch right through my long-sleeved shirt one day at the office. From then on, I considerably reduced my consumption of oranges.

By a long shot, the favorite casual meal in Melbourne was fish and chips. This delight is so popular throughout the city that specialty shops are found in every area. The fish comes wrapped in a newspaper. Our family preferred whiting, a mild ocean fish. The most important factor in the fish fry is the fat in which the fish is cooked. It has to be changed regularly or else the fish would lose its flavor.

Back in the '60s, grocery bills could be significantly reduced by shopping at bulk food markets. Sandy and I were quick to take advantage of the opportunity. We brought along our own bag for cereal or a jar for mayonnaise and stocked up at half the price.

For the most part, food in Melbourne was cheap. Thank heaven, because my pay just barely supported my family. Rent was high, as was transportation.

At sandwich shops downtown, the food selection, in my opinion, was weird. There were meat pies, sometimes made with kangaroo meat. Ugh! Wacky vegetable combinations like beets and lettuce. Another Ugh! – jaffles — whatever the hell they were. An awful-tasting spread, Vegamite, was such an Aussie favorite that we were amazed. Pizza parlors were unknown in the '60s, but they sure took over as the decades passed.

Australian Vocabulary

Since England colonized Australia and the initial settlers were British, Irish, and Scotts, much of the vocabulary and spelling traits emanated from the mother countries. The adjustment to Aussie lingo was a most interesting challenge, and in some cases, it was downright embarrassing.

There was the time when I was disciplining four-year-old Jennifer, calling out to her in the yard, "You behave yourself or I'll spank your fanny." Within minutes, the next-door neighbor was at my doorstep, and she was visibly upset. "We don't use that language here!" she reprimanded me. I was bewildered until a faculty colleague explained that in Australia, as in England, the "fanny" is the most private part of a woman's anatomy. No wonder the neighbor was upset.

In Australia, the expression "getting stuffed" can mean having sexual intercourse. When I returned from the Christmas holiday, colleague Tom Haines asked how things went. I replied, "Christmas was great. I got stuffed at dinner!" That produced a grin along with the rejoinder, "That sounds like fun—and did you have anything to eat?"

An American biscuit in Australia is a "scone." A cookie is a "biscuit." In transportation, a baby carriage is a "pram." A travel trailer is a "van or caravan."

Automotive vocabulary is particularly confusing. You couldn't even find "Auto" in the yellow pages of the phone directory. That information was classified as "Motor Car." The trunk is called the "boot." The hood is the "bonnet." The muffler is the "pong box." A car accident is a "prang."

Spelling also gave me difficulties at work. I would hand a typing assignment to Miss Lyons, the business school secretary at RMIT, and she would immediately return, abounding with criticism. "Where did you ever learn to spell?" she scolded. I bragged that in elementary school I had won a spelling award. That did not impress Miss Lyons. "Here we spell harbor 'harbour.' And honor is 'honour.' Don't you even know that aluminum is spelled—and pronounced—'aluminium?'" This banter was all in good humor—or is it humour?

In Australia, as well as in England the last letter of the alphabet is not"Zee" but is pronounced "Zed." Wow! I had some fun ribbing them about that phenomenon by saying, "Are you trying to tell me that those islands to the east of Australia are called 'New Zedland'?" They good-naturedly recognized the anomaly.

Australian Rules Football

Melbournites are sports crazy, especially when it comes to Australian Rules Football. It is an action-filled sport like no other. It seemed to me that everyone I met fanatically supported their preferred team, and the rivalry provoked arguments throughout the year. The teams are separated into several geographical areas: Essendon, Footscray, North Melbourne, Collingwood, St. Kilda, etc., each of which sponsors a team. There are also teams from other cities: Ballarat, Adelaide, Bendigo, Geelong, to name a few.

Although it is called "football," or more commonly "footie," it has little resemblance to American football. To begin with, there are no protective helmets or shoulder pads. Heads are bare, shirts and shorts are brief. And, too, there are no frequent huddles. Instead there is action-packed motion complete with body contact and thumping from the beginning of the game to the end. Photos of players usually reveal missing teeth.

Ambulances are on hand on the field perimeter, and they are frequently put into use.

Attending a game is mayhem. Most spectators stand throughout the entire contest. Fists fly; jeers and oaths abound; fights break out. When it is all over, everyone is exhausted. Then they immediately go home and watch the replay on television!

Long after the season is over, the downtown annual Moomba parade is held, and guess which floats get the most attention—those occupied with the football teams, of course. It would be like the Rose Bowl Parade having the Steelers, Packers, Patriots, Jets, and others as the main-attraction floats.

I knew I was accepted when Allen Holmes invited me to a "footie" game. Allen was an ardent Collingwood Fan. The "Magpies," the team's nickname and mascot, brought out frenzied behavior in this usually reserved fan. Standing up, sipping beers, and joining in the thunderous crowd was an exhausting experience. Allen was in a perpetual frenzy, shouting like a madman. I was taken aback by the string of oaths that came pouring out of the rough-cut woman standing in front of me.

Poisonous snakes

Ninety percent of the snakes in Australia are deadly poisonous. Children are banned from playing in grassy areas for that good reason. Once the weather warmed up sufficiently by late October, I took sons Mark and Grant for a swim in the nearby upper Yarra River. I have to confess to being obsessed with fresh water swimming, and I couldn't resist the lure of the muddy stream.

After our swim, we were walking across the grassy path leading back to the car, when a huge snake slithered across our path. It was green with yellow stripes, probably three inches through the middle and about five feet long. I found it most attractive. "Most attractive!" exclaimed colleague Jim Dyson, when I related the incident back at my RMIT office. "Mate, you're lucky to be alive. That was a tiger snake, one of the most aggressive and dangerous snakes on the whole continent of Australia! I later heard about death adders in the Outback and coral snakes in the ocean and vowed to avoid reptiles except those in glass cages.

Flies

The Australian tourist brochures seem to avoid mentioning the flies. They are ubiquitous, unrelenting, and virtually impossible to swat. It is not unusual to see people wearing netted facemasks at the beach. In summertime, they are a constantly annoying pest.

Our East Doncaster home had been built by the owner, who was installing the bathroom at the time of his split with his wife. He had installed the sink, shower, and bathtub but hadn't yet gotten around to putting in the indoor toilet. During the stay, our family had to rely on an outdoor privy. It was in a shed out in the back yard and consisted of a large 10-gallon tank. Only one tank. The Aussie term for the setup was "the dunny." Ours was a large family, and the dunny sure got used.

A man came around twice a week to empty the tank. We didn't know there was a rule regarding how far up to fill the tank. Later we learned two inches from the top was the limit. On our first Saturday in residence, the "dunny man" came early in the morning. Incredulously, he was whistling. How could someone whistle when doing that job? Apparently there was no problem that time around.

The following Wednesday while I was at work, Sandy answered a knock on the back door. It was the dunny man, and he was most upset.

"She's too full!" he sternly admonished my wife.

"What are you talking about? Sandy inquired, genuinely not knowing the cause of his wrath.

"The dunny pail. You're not supposed to let it fill up to more than two inches from the top, and yours is full to the brim!"

"What do you expect me to do?" Sandy inquired. "Do you want me to start emptying it with a ladle? And where would I put the stuff?" At that point my wife had the upper hand, because the guy had neglected to leave a spare tank just in case ours overfilled.

He grumbled something incoherent about Yanks, but he did leave an extra tank, and Lord knows how he managed to cart the overfilled one to his truck.

The Six O'clock Swill

The custom of the Six O'clock Swill has long been gone in Melbourne, but at the time our family was there, it was in full swing. By law, the bars closed at 6 p.m. It was possible to have evening outings in public where alcohol was served, but only by special permit.

I was introduced to the Swill by a few of my teaching colleagues. This get together usually occurred on a late Friday afternoon after classes. It was really quite a spectacle. A popular pub would be jammed packed with guys. No women! The beer drinking would start around 4 p.m, and the rate of consumption seemed to proceed at an accelerating pace. Australian beer had twice the alcoholic content of American beer. When the six o'clock hour approached, the bartender would announce with clarity, "Time, gentlemen!"

That was the signal to order the last of the beer before the spigot was turned off at six p.m. But patrons weren't restricted to having just one beer. Many patrons ordered half a dozen or so. The pub doors weren't locked until all of the beer had been consumed—and consumed they were, since no one could carry beer out of the barroom.

One colleague, Frank Jones, was incorrigible. He led me to some of the most popular bars in downtown Melbourne. Not that I wasn't easily led. One establishment was just across the street from the main downtown local train station on Flinders Street. The bar tender was a no-nonsense lady named Chloe. Chloe was very familiar with Frank, who was a frequent customer. She gave him a lot of leeway, but there was a limit. One Friday evening, Frank and I tested her patience. She had shut both of us off because we simply had had too much beer.

But Frank was a tiger. He urged me to join him as he went to the next bar down the street, where we each ordered a beer, and then proceeded to carry it back to the first bar, where we sat spitefully sipping the brew right within Chloe's line of vision. Within minutes, we had been dispatched out into the street. Time to call it a day.

There was some irony connected with beer drinking. Throughout the suburbs, there were sites where people were encouraged to drop off their empties. The bottle refunds were to be used for the benefit of the Boy Scouts. To me, it seemed like encouraging the healthy activities of the next generation by destroying your own health in the process.

Australian beers, as well as wines, have become popular internationally. In Melbourne, Carlton's was a favorite as was Victoria Bitter. In Perth, Swan had the best reputation, with Sydney's Foster's well in the limelight.

Those who opposed alcoholic consumption were labeled "wowsers." When I befriended a few of them, I never let on about my liquid preferences.

Our Escalating Social Life

No one made much money at RMIT. The socializing was usually done by the way of family and group get-togethers at homes. Seldom did people eat out at public restaurants back in the '60s. Franchised fast-food places were practically nonexistent.

That did not curtail the social life one whit.

It all started with a few routine beers after classes on a Friday. Since I drove my car in order to do grocery shopping at the Victoria Market downtown, I had the transportation home. Inspired by our libations, I invited teaching colleagues Howard Mitch and Rob Longton to come along to East Doncaster to meet Sandy.

Sandy had every right to be angry with the unexpected arrival of her tipsy husband and his two inebriated guests, one of whom had "chundered" (vomited) out of the car window. But she wasn't. In fact, she was pleased to meet someone new after being isolated for several weeks with little contact with anyone outside the neighborhood. She not only welcomed the Aussies; she offered them eggs, toast, and tea. I was so proud of her welcoming attitude. And the visitors were totally surprised. Australian girlfriends and wives, tired of the Friday afternoon coming-home-smashed routine, were usually hostile.

And so, because of Sandy's hospitality, the friendships began.

Harvard on the Hudson

I had brought along some photo slides we had taken back home. Several were of winter scenes with snow piled high, a sight foreign to Australians. We would invite an Australian couple in for liquid refreshments followed by a half hour or so of slides. Rob Longton, a bachelor, had been to Queensland, and he showed his pictures of the giant anthills and open spaces in that northern part of Australia. Jim Dyson had taken many photography trips to the Outback and showed slides of the stark terrain at the Flinders Range and elsewhere.

Howard Mitch and his wife came for the evening but did not bring along slides. "I hate them," Merle Mitch declared. "One time I went to a church gathering and this missionary showed hours and hours of slides taken on the island where she worked. I figured that my generous gifts to the mission were going toward purchasing film rather than providing relief, and I decided then and there never to contribute another cent!

I was particularly anxious to have Sandy meet Allen Holmes and his wife, Liz. What a successful evening we had! This time around, Sandy served a full-course dinner. I had found out that Allen had an abiding yearning for blueberry pie. That yen started years earlier in Montreal when he was stationed there with the Royal Air Force during World War II. It wasn't easy finding blueberries, but I persevered and finally located a few cans at an obscure downtown store. I also found out that Liz was partial to brandy and vermouth, mixed. Allen, of course, preferred beer.

Somehow the evening evolved into a funfest with joke telling, dancing, and frivolity. The blueberry pie was an unexpected treat for Allen, and Liz thoroughly enjoyed the brandy and vermouth. A few days afterward, Liz contacted Sandy, and she invited us to join them and their closest friends, Norm and Frieda Chipps, for an evening out at the Club Alexander, a private club downtown that featured BYOB and a nine-course dinner.

That evening at the "Club Alex" was a most memorable occasion. In between each of the nine courses—I particularly savored the oysters Fitzpatrick—there was dancing. The conversation was light and fun as we couples sipped and exchanged family experiences. It didn't take long to find out that the hurdles of bringing up young children are similar the world over. Since the Holmes's friends were all about our age, we exchanged many family experiences in the conversations.

The evening ended in a most unusual fashion. When calling it a night at the Chipps' home, Norm Chipps and I had a pissing contest right on the trunk of Frieda Chipps' favorite lemon tree. I outlasted my rival, thus becoming the champion, and so made my mark as an endeared friend to all.

Harvard on the Hudson

Toward Christmas, the business school faculty of RMIT decided to have a social celebration that was to differ markedly from previous social gatherings. In the past, it had been traditional for the guys to get together, usually on a Friday afternoon. There hadn't previously been an occasion where the wives were invited. I was very much looking forward to a party where couples attended, but some of my Australian colleagues were apprehensive.

The business faculty rented a room at the downtown Victoria Hotel, the cost (divided evenly among the guys) of which included a catered buffet dinner, booze and also a disc jockey.

Previously, colleague Bill Clermont's wife, an excellent seamstress, had offered to make Sandy a maternity dress for the occasion. It was a masterpiece.

The evening was a smashing success! Boisterous. Lots of good food, dancing, and beer. It was such a treat to find out how much fun the wives were, and they certainly weren't shy about participating in the activities. Howard Mitch added to the fun by leaping up onto a table and dancing to the applause of the crowd. Bill Clermont found his way into a closet and promptly fell asleep in the late hours of the evening. At the party, Sandy and I received many invitations for summer vacation visits. The social pace had certainly accelerated.

The Holmes had a comfortable summer home on the Mornington Peninsula, some fifty miles southeast of

Melbourne, where they took their young family for the month of January, the heart of Australian summer. Life there was casual and the pace relaxed. Fish and chips were usually picked up and brought home, and enjoying the nearby beach on Port Phillip Bay was the rule of the day.

Our family was invited along on several occasions. We parents relaxed and visited while the children reveled in the seaside experience.

There were also "Back Bay" beaches on the peninsula, but only the most daunting people — surfers, etc., spent time there. The ocean waves were formidable and threatening, the tidal currents severe, and the sharks ever-present. Naturally, I was attracted like a moth to a flame, and I experimented enough to get dashed and thrown about by the surf. Koonyah, Rye, Sorento, and Portsea beaches were likewise compellingly beautiful—and dangerous.

Vacationing While on Vacation

Adelaide and Mildura

With a reliable car on hand and a late August mid-semester break approaching, our family prepared for a two-week trip to Adelaide in the state of South Australia, some six hundred miles west of Melbourne. There were many incentives. After all, if one takes the time and spends the money to get to Australia, it would be foolish not to see as much of the country as possible while there. Like the AAA automobile club in the USA, Australia has the

Royal Auto Club, which assists in planning trips or providing assistance on the road.

Then, too, there were the inexpensive accommodations. I had been told about trailer (caravan) parks across the country, which usually featured rental caravans on site. No need to tow along your housing; just drive into a park and rent a place to stay. Some of these places were available at $4 a night! The caravans came complete with bedding and cooking utensils. All the traveler needed to supply was the food.

Packing the Wolseley for a trip with four small children was no easy challenge. We stored food on the floor between the front and back seats, clothing in the trunk. Other luggage went on the back seat. The children were to occupy a plywood shelf that stretched from the front seat to the rear window, with headroom of about 18". Several blankets were to cushion the ride. This way, the three older ones could move around or even take a nap. We thought it would be better than the discomfort of having the children wedged into the back seat in a cramped sitting position.

The Princess highway was a two-lane road in fine condition, most of the way. Sometimes it became a dirt road. Naturally, the children were bored and acted up, but they were children. Grant came upon an idea to drive his father frantic. He would scamper up the shelf until he got right near his father's ear and then do an annoying raspberry. I would take a wild swat, but I missed him time and time again. Finally, I had my fill. I kept my eye on the rear view mirror until the next scamper forward occurred. Just as Grant reached my ear, I administered a resounding belt that sent him reeling far back on the shelf.

An uncomfortable incident involved a phone call for reservations. In those days, cell phone had yet to be invented. Calling ahead required locating a pay phone, and that wasn't easy far out along the country road on which we were traveling. Finally, I spotted a roadside pub. I left the others in the Wolseley to make the phone call. It just so happened that the phone was so ancient that making a call required cranking a handle and talking to an operator. While in the process, a patron offered me a beer. It was a hot day and I accepted. I also accepted a second. At that point, Sandy's figure blocked the doorway. Boy was she upset! "You mean to tell me that you are having a beer while the five of us are out in the car broiling in the scalding sun?" she scolded. For some time, the car proceeded in silence.

What a unique experience we encountered when it came to crossing the Murray River, Australia's largest, which is wide and muddy, but not deep. We were in a remote area where no bridge had yet been built, so the car was driven onto a ferry barge and transported across the river by a cable pulley. Cool! It had grown dark, but the ferry tender beckoned the boys to get out of the car and enjoy the ride.

They were fascinated. And the guy wouldn't charge a cent for the crossing!

We arrived at the vacation town of Victor Harbor, a few miles south of Adelaide. The caravan park had everything a child would enjoy — green grass, a playground, even an ancient locomotive to climb on. Sandy fell in love with the furry baby penguins populating the wharf area. The cost of all of this? $2 a night!

Adelaide was just another bustling city, flat and uninteresting to us. We saw the main sights and hastily departed the city, backtracking toward Melbourne by using a different route.

We took a tour of a huge vineyard at the Barossa Valley. Little did we know at the time that this location was to become the heart of Australia's wine industry in the not-too-distant future.

Onward we traveled to Mildura, a country town on the Murray River in the far northern sector of the state of Victoria. Although our Australian colleagues highly recommended it as a place to see, it was a disappointment. Other than a lot of orange groves and the muddy Murray, there wasn't much else to enjoy.

The hotel we stayed at, however, was memorable. It was a huge old wooden structure, painted in bizarre colors, in the heart of the town of 15,000. Other overnight facilities weren't available. The receptionist (and owner) was truly a character. He attended the front desk in a tuxedo and tails complete with top hat. He quoted me a price that was far beyond our budget. I offered him a third of what he was asking, and the offer was hastily accepted. Downstairs, the hotel was quiet and sedate. Upstairs the young children vented their energy by tumbling and playing games in the hallways. We all slept in one room. In the morning, a gong announced the serving of a sumptuous breakfast (brekky). The owner's apparel had morphed into a white ensemble complete with apron and a chef's billowing white hat.

After breakfast, we took a flat-bottomed tour boat on the Murray, and from there we drove back to Melbourne on an uneventful several-hour trip. Oh were we glad to get back home and into our own beds! The next morning, my attention was drawn to a flat tire, which was quite a relief considering that it could have happened anytime during the 1,400-mile journey.

Canberra and Sydney

The Christmas break from RMIT gave Sandy, me, and the children an opportunity to take another motor trip. This time we headed northward to see Canberra and Sydney.

We were told not to miss the Snowy Mountain and the scheme that brought water for irrigation to extended areas of Australia, a nation that is 90% arid.

Harvard on the Hudson

What a rough ride it was on dirt mountain roads. There was that unfortunate incident involving Mt. Kosiusko, Australia's highest peak. I was most interested in driving the dirt road to the 7,000-foot summit. Sandy wasn't at all interested, and she forbade me to try. Unfortunately she dozed off when the turn-off to Kosiusko appeared ahead. I took it!

What a mistake! Up and up the old Wolseley climbed on a hazardous road that was beginning to see patches of snow. Then deeper snow. Then drifts. There were no guardrails or other protections to keep cars from going over the edge of the precipice. When it became obvious that we could proceed no further, I put the car in reverse. By this time, Sandy and the children were awake—and terrified. As I inched backward, the rear wheels began to slip off the road, threatening to plunge us into the abyss. I was inwardly frantic! For some reason, the wheels caught hold of a dry patch, and we gradually backed to safety.

Oh, was Sandy upset! A tirade of wrath regarding my stupidity reigned on me. How could I argue with that? Thence followed hours of silence.

Eventually we made it to Canberra, Australia's capital city. Canberra was developed as a compromise site between the strong political forces of Melbourne and Sydney. Previous to Canberra, Melbourne had most of the governmental activity, and Sydney was the larger and more commercial city.

The capital city was completed in 1949. World War II had temporarily halted progress for several years. Because the city was relatively new, it was as clean as a whistle. There are no overhead power lines. Homes and office buildings were new looking. Getting around the city by auto was challenging because it is designed as a series of concentric circles, as are Paris and Washington, DC. For me, a grid pattern is much easier to navigate.

The Parliament Building is constructed of white stone and surrounded by beautiful gardens. The Australian-American war monument is a very impressive spire. On display is a Japanese submarine, torn apart by depth charges while in Sydney Harbor.

We took in the sights and the following day proceeded northward to Sydney, Australia's largest city. In that city, the road system follows no pattern, sort of like Boston. Apparently the roads were built wherever the horse trails existed. We did, however, find a lovely caravan park complete with swimming pool. The offspring loved it. We spent a full day enjoying downtown Sydney. The skyline is dominated by the Harbor Bridge and the harbor itself is awesome, reputedly one of the world's most beautiful

We took the ferry across the harbor, where we were embarrassed by a spectacle that surely must have given rise to the term "Ugly American." A retired American couple was on the ferry, and she bossed him around unmercifully. "Take that picture, Earl, before it's too late!"

"Can't you ever do anything right?" "Get out of my way."
On and on. We couldn't wait to disembark at the north
side of the harbor. Our destination was the Toronga Park
Zoo, reputed to be one of the world's best. Koala bears,
kangaroos, tropical birds, and deadly poisonous black-and-
white-striped sea snakes captured our attention. It was
one exhausted family who made it back to the caravan
park that day.

Sydney is famous for its beaches. Manley Beach, on the
north side of the harbor, is most popular with the young
set. Bondi Beach, on the south shore, is actually protected
by a metal net to ward off sharks. Maroubra Beach
seemed to have the most challenging surf when we were
there. Not too far south of all this, there is a monument
commemorating the landing of Captain Cook, credited
with the discovery of Australia late in the eighteenth
century.

We decided to follow the Princess Highway southward
along the Pacific coast to get back to Melbourne. It was a
beautiful drive through grassy hillside terrain overlooking
the ocean. It took us three nights and four days. We
stopped at strange-sounding fishing villages like
Merimbula and Bermagui. Every day we spent some time
exploring beaches along the Pacific that usually featured
outcroppings of rocks buttressing the relentlessly
pounding surf.

I met my first Aboriginal, and it was a startling experience. Our car was parked near an ocean beach when a stranger approached the driver's side of the car. His skin was practically black, but his hair was bright orange. To be honest, I was really taken back until he asked, in that inimitable Australian accent, "Got a cigarette, mate?"

On the last day before arriving home, we stayed at the village of Lakes Entrance. There we walked along the 90-mile beach and saw hardly a soul.

Throughout the entire trip, we practically lived on fish and chips. Invariably, they were fresh and delicious.

The Great Ocean Road

There was one last trip away from Melbourne, and it was for a few days during the Easter holiday. Sandy chose not to join us, since baby Heather needed constant care in a more structured environment. With apprehension, I drove off with Mark, Grant, and Jennifer. I'm sure Sandy was even more apprehensive than I was.

The Great Ocean Road is a most scenic drive that runs some 90 miles southwest of Melbourne. While Australia is famous for its arid Outback attractions, nothing in my opinion can match the scenery along the Great Ocean

Road. It took some time getting to the area. The inland roads we took wound through uninteresting flatlands before approaching the sea.

Once at the sea, however, the sights were mesmerizing. Traveling westward, we first encountered the Twelve Apostles, massive sandstone monoliths projecting from the ocean floor in a windswept setting. The roadway meandered along cliffs some one hundred feet high in some places. When we were there in 1966, this had not yet become the tourist attraction that it is today. Now there is a kiosk where a fee is collected. In addition there are places to take scenic helicopter rides. It has all become too commercial.

In 1966, however, there were few spectators. I left the Wolseley at roadside and walked a narrow and dangerous path out to a great viewing sight. Photo ops of my young family enjoying the challenging terrain were irresistible—until Jennifer, age 4, damned near slipped off a ledge. That brought me back to my senses.

We traveled on to the next spectacular site, Loch Ard Gorge. In the days of sailing ships, one carrying passengers from England to Melbourne struck a reef and sank in the dead of night. Only two people of the scores on board survived, and they floated on planks into this protected cove. The ship was the "Loch Ard" and the cove was the gorge. The survivors climbed the sandstone cliffs to find their way to safety.

Several miles further along the Great Ocean Road, we stopped to marvel at the Arch, another sandstone formation. It is a huge arch some fifty feet high carved into the cliffs. Another site was named "London Bridge," which was literally a sandstone span reaching over to more sandstone formations further into the ocean. At the time, tourists could walk across the span to enjoy the view from the outer cliffs. Some years later, the span collapsed, trapping a few tourists on the far side with no way to get back to shore. Thank heaven for rescue helicopters.

On the return trip, I followed the tortuous road right along the ocean all the way back to Geelong, a large city some fifty miles south of Melbourne. We drove through the interesting villages of Apollo Bay, Lorne, and Anglesey, stopping to pick up terrific fish and chips along the way.

Our American Visitor

The children of my family called her Aunt Tell. She was neither an aunt, nor was she named Tell. Bertelle Wornham was a long-time friend of my mom's who had served as her Maid of Honor at my folks' wedding in the 1920s. That, of course, reminds me of the details I have heard of that occasion. One routine day, Tell answered her telephone to hear my mother's voice at the other end of the line asking, "Tell, what are you doing today?" Tell replied, "Esther, I have no plans." To which my mother responded, "That's good, because I want you to serve as my Maid of Honor at four o'clock this afternoon. Arthur and I are getting married!" And that's how it went.

Bertelle had remained single and had served as the librarian for the Rensselaer school system until she retired in 1965. Over the years, she had traveled throughout the USA by car and also on cargo ships to worldwide destinations during her summer vacations.

All through our growing years, Aunt Tell had watched over us like a godmother, remembering each of us at Christmas with a fine book. She seemed always to be kindly and in good spirits. And speaking of spirits, she thoroughly enjoyed the conviviality of interesting conversation, particularly in the company of friends over some bourbon and water or maybe even a martini. She seldom overdid it, however.

Sandy and I were delighted when she wrote to say she was hoping to visit us in Melbourne. It would be so good to talk about goings on back in upstate New York and to reminisce over years past. We met her at the airport and then drove her to the Hotel Victoria in downtown Melbourne, where she planned to stay for a few days.

The next morning we picked her up at the hotel and drove around to see some sights: some lovely gardens, the Healesville Sanctuary — a mini-zoo featuring emus, duck-billed platypus, kangaroos, koalas, etc. Since Aunt Tell had planned to stay for several days, the inconvenience of driving into the city to meet her didn't make sense.

"Why don't you just move in with us during your stay," Sandy suggested. "It would give us more time to spend together and would surely save on the time spent driving back and forth."

Tell at first refused because she had seen our cramped household. We knew we could borrow a cot from Bud Johnson. After continued persuasion, however, Tell changed her mind. "Alright, I'll stay with you but with two conditions: that we stop and pick up some alcoholic beverages and that I pay for my share of the food." The deal was settled. We stopped at a liquor store and stocked up on the way back to East Doncaster.

That's another Australian attraction, the "Drive By" liquor store. It is so convenient to drive up to the window, order, pay, and drive away. With a glass of sherry on the outside porch in the evening before supper, we became one happy threesome.

Since Aunt Tell was with us, we took her along to the beach at Mornington when we visited with the Holmes. She was so taken in by our Australian friends that she insisted upon treating us to dinner at the swanky Southern Cross hotel in downtown Melbourne.

"I don't care for the place," said Miss Lyons, the secretary back at RMIT. "Why not?" I inquired. "It's just too American," she responded with her knowing glint.

Harvard on the Hudson

What a night we had at dinner! Brandy seemed to be the order of the evening. We each had four or five of them before dinner came to a close. Apparently it found its way into Aunt Tell's cranium, because her reaction was most unexpected.

"I want to tell you about my retirement party," she announced. She then expanded upon the event, using hand gestures and voice inflections to emphasize the story. Apparently, she was somewhat annoyed by her parting gift from her career at the library — a Lifetime Achievement Memorial Scholarship. "It struck me as an old-age commemoration," she explained. The Holmes and Sandy and I listened with amusement, admiring the fun details in Aunt Tell's presentation.

Within minutes of completing her story, Aunt Tell said, "I want to tell you about my retirement party." From then on she repeated, word for word, gesture for gesture, every detail she had previously talked about. Apparently, the booze had kicked in.

At first Sandy and I and our Australian friends listened thoughtfully. When it became obvious what was going on, we could no longer contain ourselves. I looked at Allen, and he was laughing so much that tears were running down his cheeks. Elizabeth leaned over to me and whispered, "Haven't we heard this before?" That did it! It was all Sandy and I needed to start our shoulders shaking while trying to contain ourselves.

After dinner, we took the elevator to ground level and proceeded toward the Holmes' car. I took Aunt Tell's arm to guide her. She resisted, "I can manage perfectly well by myself," she huffed. When I let go of her arm, she gradually veered to the left and eventually bumped into a brick wall. More laughter from the group!

What a grand lady was Aunt Tell. Before we left the Holmes, she invited them to come to America and to stay as long as they liked at her home. She said she would probably be traveling and that they would have the place to themselves. And, by golly, a few years later, the Holmes family took advantage of her offer.

Farewells

The remaining months flew by so quickly. Soon, however, the cold and wet weather began to roll back in. I had an interesting conversation about the weather in Melbourne while talking with a retired educator during an interview.

"Our wet, cold weather seems to come from Tasmania to the south of us," he said. "The dry weather comes in from Adelaide in the west, and the windy, hot weather comes down from the north from Sydney. " I pondered his remarks.

"From what you are saying, it sounds as if Melbourne doesn't have any weather of its own," I said. "Is that the way you see it?" He thought that was a great observation.

Harvard on the Hudson

In spite of the close friendships our family had developed, we looked forward to our return to upstate New York. The packing process once again took place. There was a farewell party put on by the staff at RMIT, and we had one great but tearful time bidding our farewells.

So many of the Aussies were there at Essendon aerodrome (that's the way the Aussie's say it) to say goodbye. We hugged, shook hands, cried a lot, and finally took our departure.

It had never occurred to me when setting out from home that we would make so many close friends in a foreign land. We loved them so much that we returned four times before age-related infirmities took their toll.

CHAPTER TEN – REVISITING AUSTRALIA; AND ON AROUND THE WORLD

In 1978 there was a second trip to Australia. I had received a sabbatical from Hudson College, a half year at full pay to study contemporary developments in college classroom computerized accounting education. I was to visit 30 colleges and universities in locations all around the world. It was a dream sabbatical!. The eventual benefit to the college was the establishment of a heavily enrolled computer software course for business and liberal arts majors.

The sabbatical just happened to coincide with my two older sons' completion of secondary school. Grant and Mark would be free to travel with me before joining the Navy upon returning home. The boys, aged 18 and 17, were as free as birds and anxious to head off; that was until a few days before departing when each fell hopelessly in love with the minister's daughters. Once day, Dad was a hero for planning the world trip. Weeks later I became an ogre for stifling their hormonal desires. By then, it was too late for them to back out. The flight tickets were already purchased. We would first fly to California and then make a stopover in Tahiti. After that, we would fly to New Zealand and then touch down in Australia for a four-month stay with the friends we had made there. From Australia, we would continue on around the world until we would meet up with Sandy and the other five children in Europe and proceed on an "idyllic" travel-van vacation around Europe – with stops at colleges and universities all along the way.

It all sounded so promising, but there were sure to be pitfalls right from the outset. The boys and I left our upstate New York home on a blustery, snowy day. Sandy had fire in her eyes when she bid adieu to her strong, healthy husband and sons—and then continued shoveling the white stuff as we drove off.

San Diego Stopover

Having charge of two young men in their late teens can be a challenge. Once on the flight out of Albany heading for California the suggestions began with me trying to fend them off as best I could because I knew their mother would find out and I'd be in hot water.

The first trial came when we reached Los Angeles and went to the rental car kiosk. "Dad, let's take that one!" Grant urged. He pointed out a bright orange Pontiac Firebird that looked as though it was hurtling through space even though it was stationed in the parking lot.

"I know this kid and I know his interest is *speed*, but how do I deter him without seeming too much like an old killjoy," I mused.

Upon closer inspection, I found an excuse. The trunk space was barely sufficient to hold a shoebox, let alone the traveling luggage we had brought with us.

"Sorry, Grant, there's just not enough room in the trunk," I reasoned and then proceeded to put a medium-sized Mercury on my charge card.

Southward we drove to San Diego for a respite of a few days before flying off to Australia.

Our San Diego stopover involved staying with good friends, the Wormans. The boys and I would stay at the home of 40-year-old Tim Worman and his wife. They lived in LaJoya, not far from the elderly World War II General, Tim Worman Sr. (brother of Aunt Tell), and his wife, Lottie, who were ensconced in a nearby condo.

The retired general proved to be a real curmudgeon, gruff and opinionated, but deep inside he had a great sense of humor. In World War II, he was loved by his troops.

Harvard on the Hudson

When meeting the General, I had prepared myself to break the ice. I'd been reading about the Pacific theater where the General had served. One of the heroes of the time was a General Shoup of the US Marines. I was correct in thinking that these two generals, Shoup and Worman, had known each other, since they served in the same area. I assumed they were good friends.

"Were you a good friend of General Shoup," I inquired of the General after being introduced.

"Shoup? I hated the son-of-a bitch!" he replied. Thence followed silence. I quickly changed the topic.

Lottie Worman, the General's wife, was, in a word, chatty. As a matter of fact, she simply could not stop talking. Much of what she said was pure, unadulterated blather. It was soon obvious that the General completely tuned her out.

On the second evening, the entire party, Wormans and Stevens, ate at a Mexican restaurant. This was a first experience for the Stevens. Mexican food hadn't yet become popular in upstate New York. Our hosts insisted upon treating.

I was absolutely bowled over by the menu. I didn't recognize one single appetizer, entrée, or dessert. Rather than stabbing at a choice, I asked the General—after a cocktail or two—, "Just what is an enchilada?"

"Don't ask me," the retired war hero responded. "When it comes to Mexican food, I don't know my ass from a green tomato." That broke the ice, and it really tickled Mark and Grant.

While at dinner, we agreed that the General and Lottie would take us on a tour of Camp Pendleton, the Marine base over which General Worman had charge just previous to retirement. He and Lottie picked us up the following morning. As we rode to the base, Lottie never stopped talking, noting this and that point of interest.

Eventually they pulled up to the main gate. The General, of course, had a pass, and we drove onto the base. Abruptly, the General stopped the car. "I have something to say," he announced. He barked at his wife, "Lottie, I want you to shut your god-damned mouth while I tell the boys what they are seeing."

There was dead silence. I sat in the back seat between the boys, and I could feel them shaking with laughter.

"Why, General," Lottie gasped, "You shouldn't use language like that in front of the young people. Of course I'll stay quiet while you give the tour."

She became quiet—for a minute or so. After that, she began blabbering about what we were seeing: "And here is where the General and I stayed — and there is the recreation hall — and over there is the main parade ground, etc." For the General, it was a losing proposition. For us, it was just plain fun.

Naughty Things to See

"Dad," Grant suggested, "We'd like you to take us to a strip joint."

"Oh, no," I responded, "I'd like to, but sooner or later your mother would find out about it, and I'd be in deep shit."

That was my initial reaction. Inside I thought, "What's the big deal. They'll see that stuff sooner or later somewhere along the line."

So on our last night in town, I searched out a strip joint, not telling the boys where they were going. It was around midnight, and I located a hot spot without any trouble. Wanting to be cautious, I asked the boys to wait in the car while I scoped out the scene.

When I tried to open the barroom door, it was jammed. I pushed harder and found the cause of the obstruction: a human being lying prone on the floor with blood seeping onto the carpet. The music was blaring, the booze was flowing, and a fight had broken out. I stepped back outside, closed the door behind me, and headed back to the car.

"Sorry, boys," I said. "That place was a little too rough. Maybe some other time."

Tahiti

Our first stopover outside of the USA was Tahiti. At the airport, we rented a car and drove out into the country to a touristy village of thatched-roof huts located right on the beach. At the time, all flights to Tahiti from the USA arrived there at 2 a.m., an exhausting time of night following a seven-hour flight. Once we found our hut, we crashed for a long sleep.

The following morning, Mark awakened me. He and Grant had gotten up earlier and headed for the beach. "Dad, you have come and see what's going on down on the beach." I followed Mark out of the hut. There on the beach were dozens of lovely looking ladies—all topless! At last, the boys had gotten their wish to see nude women, and I was off the hook.

Tahiti was hot and sultry. The snorkel swimming on the main island was awesome, with so many brilliantly colored fish around the coral reefs. Some years later, Sandy and I visited the main island of Tahiti and were disappointed to note that most of the colorful fish had disappeared. Pollution had taken its toll. However, she and I ventured on to the nearby island of Moorhea, and there, once again, I marveled at the colorful fish in abundance.

Harvard on the Hudson

New Zealand

The boys and I arrived at Auckland Airport, probably the cleanest one we were to see on the entire round-the-world trip. We limited our travels to the North Island, stopping at the University of Auckland and the Wellington Technical College to see what was going on in computerized classrooms. Along the way, we visited the Glow Worm caves, sulfuric-smelling Rotarura, examples of the Maori culture, windy and hilly Wellington, and finally, New Plymouth, where we arose in the morning spellbound by the sight of majestic and symmetrical Mount Egmont in the distance.

The New Zealand stopover took five thoroughly interesting and enjoyable days. By that time, however, we were ready to stop over for four months in Melbourne.

Australia

It had been nearly thirteen years since I'd last seen Australia. At that time, Mark and Grant were only eight and seven years old. Now they were teenagers, full of piss and vinegar. Our friends, the Allen Holmes family in Melbourne, had insisted that we stay with them for the four months while in Australia. I jumped at the invitation.

The Holmeses had a lovely ranch home in the suburbs of Melbourne, and they also had a beach house down on the Mornington Peninsula. I thought it would be a great idea to spend most of the week at the beach and give both the Holmes and us some privacy. Our hosts had close friends who generously offered us the use of their daughter's VW bug while their daughter was traveling in Europe.

The four months went by all too fast. I visited more than twenty colleges and universities, learning more and more about computer classroom use. This was way back when punch cards were in vogue. At one institution, the students would punch in their computerized assignment, and the instructor would collect them and send them to a different institution, where a mainframe computer processed the assignment. In a few days, the punched cards would be returned to the instructor who, in turn, gave them back to the students. This was a time-consuming process, because those were the days before personal computers would make transactions immediate.

At some of the colleges, I was asked to give a talk to the business faculty about developments on campuses in the USA. On one occasion, the talk was delivered in a small faculty lounge holding a dozen or so instructors. It took place just after lunch. Big mistake! I thought I was doing fine until I heard the distinct sound of snoring. I spied the guilty instructor, a young man who had his head tilted back on the backrest of the chair with drool running out of his gaping mouth. Talk about bringing someone back to reality! I quickly brought the presentation to a close.

At the Holmes' Melbourne residence, the accommodations were somewhat cramped. Son Grant bunked in with the Holmes' son Rich in a basement bedroom, and Mark and I slept in separate single beds in the guest room. That's when I learned that Mark insisted upon sleeping in a totally soundless room. No clocks, no distractions of any kind for him. Unfortunately I had a snoring habit, and it was driving Mark bonkers. The boy finally hit upon a solution. He would take his tennis racket to bed with him, and when my snoring commenced, he would stretch over and belt me with the racket. After a few of those wounding blows, I learned to stop snoring!

During the week, the boys and I would go to the beach to enjoy watching the surf, living like bachelors and stuffing ourselves with fast foods. After so many years since our last visit to Melbourne, the city had become quite cosmopolitan due to the huge influx of southern Europeans and Asians. Now there were pizza shops and Asian cuisine throughout the metropolitan area.

The Holmes's boy, Richard, was in a rock band that sounded terrible, but it brought in teenage friends and a chance for Mark and Grant to get away from the adults.

During those four months, we traveled around extensively, both for research work and for pleasure. Visiting the Great Ocean Road sandstone formations was yet again an awesome experience. Seeing kangaroos on the golf courses at Anglesey and attending cricket matches made the time fly by.

In no time at all, the four months were over, and we flew off to our next destinations, Singapore and Indonesia.

Singapore

The plane touched down at Singapore, where we had scheduled a three-day respite.

The island nation of Singapore is located just about on the equator. Consequently it is hot and muggy most of the time. It has to be one of the cleanest and highly regulated cities in the world. There is a $5 charge if you are caught spitting out gum. Taxi fares are strictly regulated by close inspection of meters.

Bargaining is the customary way to do business. Stocking up on souvenirs meant visiting several shops and comparing prices. It was fun.

We did it up right by staying at Raffles Hotel, the center of pride for the British Empire when it controlled the island nation and also the Straits of Malacca.

Incidentally, Raffles is where the Singapore Sling, once a very popular cocktail, was first concocted. The combination of sloe gin and 7-up made a delightful drink. But pricing was a haphazzard situation. When I ordered one in my room, it was $3. At the hotel restaurant it was $4 and in the bar, $5. Wouldn't one think that the cheapest drink price would be at the bar where the drink is prepared?

While in Singapore, I visited a technical college and then it was off with the boys on a sightseeing tour followed by hours in the hotel pool.

Indonesia

Sandy and I had some years ago befriended a couple, Bart and Ilana Wyman, who had since moved to Jakarta. He became the principal of an American school and his wife taught French. It seemed only sensible for us to stop by for a few days as a part of our globe-circumventing sojourn.

What a culture shock! For the first time I found myself in a third-world nation, teeming with people. I was handicapped by being totally unfamiliar with the native language. Jakarta was designed for a full capacity of about two million souls, but there were eight million living there at the time. The canals throughout the city were used for irrigation, drinking water, and sewerage for the natives. No wonder the average life span was 35 years, what with the bacteria in the water supply.

The Wymans occupied a lovely villa far out in the country. Their lifestyle was enviable, with a chauffeur, cook, and housekeepers all in a lush tropical setting. They were excellent hosts, meeting us at the airport, driving us to see interesting sights, doing some native restaurant hopping, etc. We had the time of our lives. Bart even asked the boys along on his Hash Harry routine, an orienteering run with several of his buddies followed by a few cold beers.

I had a most memorable experience while there. I had taken up the habit of having a tablet and pen on the nightstand next to my bed so that, if something relating to my research came to me in the middle of the night, I could turn on the lamp and write it down.

One night I was sleeping soundly when a great idea came to me. I turned on the light and reached for the writing materials. As I was taking down notes, I happened to look up at the bedroom ceiling. It was completely covered with tiny lizards! "I never noticed that before," I thought to myself. "What an interesting and peculiar wallpaper pattern!"

Then something unnerving happened. One lizard dropped from the ceiling onto the bed. Then another. And another. And then more. I was horrified beyond belief. What to do? With resignation, I bravely turned off the light, adjusted to my favorite reclining position, and went back to sleep. Oddly, in the morning my little bedmates had disappeared!

Harvard on the Hudson

Sri Lanka

When I was young, geography was one of my favorite subjects. I'd read about Ceylon, that pendant of an island just south of India. It just so happened that it was on the way, so we planned a five-day stopover. The visit to Indonesia had caused considerable culture shock. Sri Lanka, formerly Ceylon, was equally fascinating, but this time around we had no friends waiting to guide us.

We arrived in Colombo, the capital, in the middle of the night. Our taxi took us along darkened streets that we shared with oxcarts guided by barefooted natives.

"What in the world have I us gotten into?" I pondered, fearing that at any moment we might be dragged from the cab, robbed, and assaulted. We were finally deposited at a dimly-lit hotel, replete with dark red wallpaper and with beaded curtains at every entranceway.

In the morning, I rejoiced that we were still alive and safe and that a tourist agent had his office in the hotel. Was he a piece of work! Darkly complected and with a beard, turban, and flowing robe, he talked slowly in a low voice. "What can I do to help you?" he inquired in a most sinister tone.

I had thought about an itinerary whereby I could hire a taxi for five days, tour the island's most interesting sights, and stay at hotels complete with meals.

"How much would such an adventure cost me?" I inquired.

The mysterious man pondered and answered, "Five hundred dollars."

I responded, "I really don't have that much money available to spend."

The agent said, "Then how much money do you have available?"

"One hundred fifty dollars," I offered.

The agent thought a while before he told me that we could have the entire tour package for five days for one hundred fifty dollars. "It sure pays to bargain in this culture," I later told the boys.

"One more thing," the agent said. "I would like you to be my agent in New York City for selling star sapphires. Do you know that Sri Lanka has every precious gem with the exception of opals?" I was totally unaware of that fact.

The mysterious man tried to further lure me into becoming his agent by bringing out a display of what he purported to be star sapphires. "Look closely. See the white cross in the middle of the jewel? That indicates that it is truly a star sapphire. I studied the beautiful red stone, but confessed, "Look, I'd be the worst sales agent you could ever have. I wouldn't know a star sapphire from a red beer mug." That concluded the interview.

The five-day adventure around the island nation of Sri Lanka couldn't have been more interesting. Sacred shrines, Buddhist temples, monkeys, working elephants, wild elephants, domesticated elephants, coconuts, pineapples, cinnamon, nutmeg, bananas, rubber plantations, tea plantations, natives planting rice in terraces, water buffalo—the country had it all. Our cab driver, Prada, was an amiable young man who smoked one cigarette after another.

Our hotel stays were interesting. Prada would carry our luggage to the door and then disappear until we were ready to go to the next place of interest. There was a tourist section of the hotels and an adjoining area where the guides stayed. There was also a two-tiered cost structure where the tourists paid a substantial price for lodging and food, and the guides paid a much lower rate.

There were some primitive customs. The hotel "laundry" consisted of an area on the river shore where the employees washed the clothes and beat them dry on the rocks. All along most roads were donkey and oxen carts for carrying produce, grain, etc. Working elephants lugged heavy logs. In some areas, the roads were crowded by hundreds of people walking to and from their destinations. There were few cars but thousands of bicycles.

One point of interest was the setting where the movie, "The Bridge over the River Kwai" was filmed. The river was still there but the bridge itself had been detonated during the filming. Still, the guide was able to point to the reinforcement rods imbedded in the rocks where the bridge once towered over the stream. In a small kiosk were on-the-movie-set photos of Alec Guinness and William Holden, two of the film's stars.

Tea bushes abounded. Everywhere native Sri Lankans were plucking the tea leaves and dropping them into sacks suspended from their shoulders. Huge sheds for drying the tea dotted the hilltops.

Rubber was collected somewhat like maple syrup. A slash was made in the trunk of the tree, and the sap dripped into small coconut shells. I took a photo of Grant stretching a long sinew of rubber held by several Sri Lankan children.

There were snake charmers along the roadside at some villages. The cobras stood upright, hoods flared, using a basket as a base while the charmer played his flute-like instrument. I suspected that the snakes had been defanged but wasn't about to ask. I lay on my stomach to get a close up of a menacing-looking cobra from a few feet's distance. That's when the damned snake slithered out of the basket and came toward this foolish American tourist with the camera. And that is when this American tourist with the camera made a dash for it back to the taxi!

I treated my sons to a ride on an elephant. It was a very young elephant, and all three of us were placed on its back. I noted with interest that the elephant had a lot of spiny hair. As we disembarked, the begging process ensued. The fellow who lured us to take a ride put out his palm saying, "Please sir, a little something for the owner of the elephant." Following that, another palm, "Please sir, a little something to pay for food for the elephant." Following that, yet another outstretched palm "for the man who took your picture when you were riding the elephant." And still another "for the little boy who takes care of the elephant." Whenever a palm was greased, another reached out. And another and another and another. Finally, Prada came to our rescue and hustled us into the taxi.

The five fascinating days in Sri Lanka passed by in a flash. I, who have traveled in several countries over my lifetime, recall those days in Sri Lanka as the most interesting of all of my travels. What a shame that a year or so after our visit, Sri Lanka was torn apart by a civil war that lasted for decades.

India

The next leg of our journey took us to Bombay (now Mumbai) India. The two-day stopover was downright depressing. To begin with, as we awaited an airport cab to take us to our hotel, a fistfight broke out between two cab drivers. One had butted the lineup with his cab in order to get our ride. The cabdriver who was properly in line to get us flew out of his vehicle, and fists were immediately flying.

Along the streets were people in desperate physical straits. There were the blind and those with severed limbs. Hundreds had running sores. All were begging for alms. In the shadowed areas under the towering arch, the Gateway to India, there were starving souls lying on the sidewalk. After one overnight stay we flew off to Cairo, Egypt.

Egypt

Our plane touched down in Cairo in the wee hours of the morning when it was still pitch black. We were hot and tired and out of sorts and not at all expecting our poor treatment. A young teenager rudely grabbed our luggage right out of our hands and took it to an awaiting cab, begging for "baksheesh" (a handout) all the way. We were driven to the hotel "El Nil" (The Nile) on the bank of the famous river.

Upon arising, I went to the bathroom to pour myself a glass of water. Big mistake! What came out of the faucet was darker than black coffee, an immediate warning. Since Coke was made using boiled water, we went that route. In spite of our precautions, somewhere or other Grant acquired an intestinal bacterial infection that was to make him extremely ill by the time we reached Switzerland.

At the hotel, the meals were pricey, and we travelers had no idea how to read the menu.

I tried patiently to make a phone call for my appointment at the University of Cairo about a mile from our hotel. Placing the call took at least forty-five minutes! I took a cab to the appointment, where I had a most interesting visit with the professor of accounting. "We have no computers," he admitted. "Teaching is impossible here. Lecture halls hold 2,000 students. Many of them are fidgeting and coughing, so it makes it impossible for the others to hear." I was relieved when the interview ended so that I could get back to the boys.

Along the boulevards, there were hundreds of donkey carts carrying watermelons!

As we strolled along the street, our hunger pangs grew. We were afraid, however to touch anything on sale because we simply didn't know what it was. Some black meat hung from racks at outdoor markets. "It might be some version of salami, but I'm not taking the chance," I thought to myself.

Along the streets were dozens of uniformed armed military personnel. It was most unsettling.

It was impossible for us to get around the city by bus because the bus signs were in Arabic. We were forced to hail a cab and, of course, were fleeced accordingly.

A visit to the pyramids is a must for tourists, and so we rented a cab to travel to Giza not far from Cairo. Once there, we were approached by a man of the desert complete with white headdress and flowing robe.

"I am Abdul and I am at your service. In what way can I help you?" he asked in fractured English.

"We'd like to see the pyramids," I said.

"I will make your visit a memorable one," said Abdul. "We will see the pyramids on camelback, but first you must pay the fee." For the first of many, many times that day, Abdul held out his outstretched palm and I felt my wallet grow thinner. Such payments are called baksheesh in much of the Arab world. It was to become an integral part of my vocabulary over the next few hours.

What came lumbering toward us from the stable area didn't look at all like camels but very much like horses instead! I just shook my head. I had an inkling that this was to be an endless rip-off, and I was right on target.

Harvard on the Hudson

Then we and Abdul rode out into the desert. Not more than five minutes had passed before Abdul had us stop near a small kiosk manned by a very young boy.

"The horses are very tired, and I hope you would be willing to come up with something to help pay for their feed," Abdul said, holding out his palm. I complied with the request.

Abdul was just gaining his stride. "And perhaps you have something for the little boy. He works very hard in the hot sun." I again came forth with some baksheesh.

Further along, Abdul again interrupted our tour by stopping us and saying, "Sir, I have a large family, and I do not make much money on my job as a guide. Could you spare a little something to feed my family?" More baksheesh.

Eventually we approached the Sphinx. In the background was a huge pyramid. Abdul held out his hand again. "Good sir, let me take your camera and get a picture of you and your sons near the sphinx," he said. Once more, I came through with baksheesh. At this point, every time Abdul asked for more money, the boys couldn't help but laugh. I, however, did not at all appreciate the continuous begging.

We approached one of the pyramids. We were surprised that many of the cut stones from which the ancient wonders were built were much smaller than we were led to believe. Some of the rocks were about two feet square.

In the movie "The Ten Commandments," director Cecil DeMille had Charlton Heston (Moses), along with a dozen extras straining their guts out to move huge blocks.

The blocks of stone comprising the outer part of the pyramid were in steps. I knew what was coming next and this time I was prepared.

"Would you like to climb the pyramid?" Abdul inquired.

I fired back, "Not on your life. I know that you will want baksheesh to get us up there and more baksheesh to get us back down!"

We proceed back toward the embarkation area on horseback. Once again, Abdul stopped the horses.

By this time, I was thoroughly fed up. "Don't ask for more money, Abdul. You really should be ashamed of yourself, continuously panhandling your customers day in and day out!" My voice had risen in pitch. Suddenly the humor of the whole ordeal struck me, and my fury changed to laughter. Unexpectedly, Abdul joined in the hilarity of the ridiculous situation.

The outburst didn't deter him, however. When we eventually climbed down from our horses, Abdul approached us once more with his palm out. "Would you please consider a tip, sir?" he inquired.

Like a fool, I complied.

Harvard on the Hudson

The following day we flew to Athens.

Greece

We spent only two overnights in Athens. That gave us time enough to stroll around the Placka and to pay a late-afternoon visit to the Acropolis, visiting the ruins of the Parthenon and other sights.

In the evening, we returned to the Acropolis to enjoy the Sound and Light Show, which featured the lighted ruins and an excellent narrative involving the "Cradle of Democracy." In the audience, however, was a loud-mouthed Texan who would be an additional embarrassment to the reputation of American tourists.

"George, isn't this fascinating?" the Texan's 60ish wife commented. He bellowed: "Nothing but a pile of rocks to me." Class!

On the final day in Greece, I noticed a physical change in Grant. He was becoming listless and he wanted to rest continually.

More of Europe

It had been pre-arranged before leaving upstate New York that Sandy and the five younger children would fly to Luxembourg, where they would meet up with the boys and me. From there, we would tour several European countries by travel van.

I had made the arrangements for the travel van while in Australia. It fell far short of Sandy's expectations. The one I rented was designed to comfortably transport a group of five. I thought that we could squeeze in the nine family members during the daytime travel. Because of such limited sleeping accommodations, we would have to find somewhere for four or five to sleep each night.

The boys and I flew in from Greece and proceeded to hire the travel van. In a few hours, the Icelandic Airlines plane landed and off came the five other family members. There ensued a joyous but brief reunion.

Then Sandy saw the van. She was expecting spacious accommodations instead of the small box in the parking lot.

"Is this it?" she asked me in disbelief. There was a chill in the air as we crammed ourselves into what was to be our transportation and living quarters for the next month.

"But honey, it has a refrigerator, a shower and a range," I meekly offered as a consolation." Silence greeted me. What was worse, by the time we reached England the butane fuel tank ran out, and propane—unusable as a substitute— was the only fuel available. Thus went the possibility of cooking and showering in the travel van as long as we were in England.

We started out by driving through Germany, Switzerland, Holland, Belgium, and France on the mainland. By the time we reached Switzerland, Grant's condition had deteriorated to the extent that he didn't want to get out of bed. Something had to be done and soon. In the afternoon of our overnight in Lucerne, I found a hospital and took Grant there. Not one person in the hospital spoke English. The staff and professional people only spoke German. We had to employ some ingenuity to apprise the doctor of my son's ailment. I pointed to Grant, who rubbed his stomach, grimaced, and with a pained expression, squatted on the office floor, while making defecation grunts.

The doctor caught the communication immediately. He gave us a few pills. The next morning Grant was cured. Wonderful!

I visited a technical college in Liege, Belgium, and two others in Holland.

To find a place to stay each night, we had bought a travel van guide to overnight lodgings and campsites. Sometimes the travel guide was in error or outdated. For instance, we had planned to stay at a campsite outside of Paris. When we got there, we discovered that there had been so much rain in the recent past that the campsite had washed away down the Seine. Instead, we drove onward to downtown Paris, passing under the Arch de Triumph and on to a small hotel in the city.

We had planned it so that one night, four of us would stay at a hotel and the other five would sleep in the van. The next night, those who had stayed at the hotel the previous night would get to sleep in the van. It worked out satisfactorily most of the time.

In Paris, we viewed the Eiffel Tower, Versailles, the Louvre, and the jail where Marie Antoinette had been imprisoned before she was taken to the guillotine. I didn't realize until too late that the tourist guide would speak only in French. We had no idea what the fellow was saying, but we got the hint when he drew his finger across his throat after mentioning Marie Antoinette.

I had heard that the French were unfriendly to Americans. It turned out to be just the opposite for us, probably because our group was a small, young family. We were the recipients of smiles and other friendly favors no matter where we went.

All of the family proved to be great traveling companions with the exception of Giss, who was one continuous pain in the neck. At age eleven, she didn't want to go in the first place. It was summer, and she wanted to stay home with her friends. She was determined not to have a good time, and she was very successful. Fortunately, the rest of the brood ignored her.

When in Holland, we took the rare opportunity to spend a morning at a cheese testing ceremony. The entire square in the center of town was filled with foot-round Edam cheeses. The inspections took place only on Fridays, and we were lucky to be in that area at the time.

All of us bounded out of the travel van except Giss. I implored her to join us. "I'm not coming. I'm staying in the van," she insisted. "Who wants to see a bunch of cheese?" And so she missed the event.

At another attraction, there were some 80 acres of tulips to behold. They would be shipped out to places throughout the world. Giss adamantly remained in the van, using the excuse that she couldn't find her comb.

"I'll lend you mine," her sister Jenn volunteered.

"No thanks," said Giss, "I don't want to catch your bugs."

And then there was the visit to Westminster Abbey in London. For some reason, I had always been interested in Mary, Queen of Scots, and wanted to see her tomb. The family walked the corridors of the building, searching for the tragic queen's final resting place. The searching went on and on until Giss dug in her toes and abruptly sat down on a patch of grass in one of the sanctuary's quiet garden areas.

"I'm not goin' another step," she stubbornly announced. "I'm sick of wandering around lookin' for some old grave you can't find." She directed her frown at me. And then she said, "If you didn't know where you were going, why did you bring us here?"

Inside, I couldn't blame her, but I wouldn't admit it. How do you explain to an eleven-year-old that even the best of travelers get lost? Fortunately, around the next corner we found the sought-after plaque.

On rare occasions, Giss would come around to enjoying herself, but she didn't let the rest of the family know it.

The travel van died in England after we had left London and were driving toward Bath. The engine thermometer had registered high since leaving Luxembourg. I would stop periodically to add water, but that only temporarily eased the problem. There must have been a water leak from the engine block. The vehicle broke down on a busy stretch of highway, and it took several hours for help to arrive on the scene. We had to be towed to a garage in the town of Maidenhead. For some reason, there were few complaints from the family, and I was really proud of them.

We found a country estate hotel where we would be ensconced for five days, waiting for the engine to be replaced. Fortunately, it was a rental vehicle, and according to the rental contract, the repair and the lodging would be completely taken care of.

I had to make several angry calls to Luxembourg, but it all turned out well, except that we lost several days of the itinerary, and I had to cancel a few academic appointments. To balance it off, however, the weather was sunny and warm and there was a swimming pool nearby.

Once back on the road, we traveled to the University of Lancaster in England's beautiful northwest Lakes country. The only night in that area, the four oldest offspring stayed in a B&B while the rest of us slept in the van. In the morning, I drove to the B&B to pick up Mark, Grant, Jenn, and Giss.

The landlady was as cross as a bear when I arrived at the door. "That one can never stay here again," she said, shaking her finger in Mark's direction. I recoiled in disbelief. Mark, the oldest, was the most mild mannered of the entire family. What could he have done wrong?

"He slept in three different beds," she scowled. "Now I have to do an extra pile of linens just because of him." I paid the overnight rent and hastily loaded the four into the van.

"Why on earth would you sleep in three different beds?" Sandy angrily asked Mark.

His response was purely out of the pages of "Goldilocks." "The first bed she showed me was too soft so I went to another. That one was too hard, but the third was just right." How could anyone stay angry after that confession?

I next had an appointment at the University of Leeds. From there, we drove across the moors for an overnight at Scarborough before driving up to Newcastle where, travel van and all, we boarded an overnight ocean-going ferry to Bergen, Norway.

It was on the ferry that I met a congenial young Scot who was taking a respite from working on an offshore oil well. He was ready to relax, and he wanted me to join him. "You must get used to aquavit, Norway's favorite drink," he explained, and with that he produced a flask. Sandy was bedding down the children at the time, so I joined him for a drink, and then another, and then another.

When Sandy caught up with me, I was lying face down on the deck of the ferry with my most prized possessions—wallet, camera, watch, and glasses—placed neatly in a row next to me. The next day was another of those quiet ones.

Driving in Norway was one continuous challenge after another. Narrow roads, mountains, tunnels (some unlit), fjords, and ferries. Somehow we navigated some three hundred miles northward to the city of Alesund, where we stayed at a rented home arranged for us by a great family friend, Lifden, who some time earlier had come to upstate New York to spend several months with my older brother.

It rained on and off for our five-day stay, but Lifden made the visit a terrific experience. And then we drove on to another nearby city, Andlesness, where we visited with the parents of our Norwegian sister-in-law. What an interesting experience! None of the Norwegians spoke English, and none of us spoke Norwegian, so the visit consisted of eating delicious snacks, sipping coffee, and a lot of looking at photos and nodding and smiling.

After our brief stay in Andlesness, we drove southward through Sweden and then across the channel to Denmark. A brief stopover in Copenhagen gave us a chance to visit the Mermaid of the Sea and what was advertised as the original of its kind, Tivoli Gardens, where the offspring expended their pent-up energy on a variety of rides and contests.

From Denmark, it was more southward travel through Germany and eventually back to Luxembourg where we boarded the Icelandic Airway flight back to New York City.

W. L. Staats

Iceland

The family had one last scheduled stopover. Icelandic Airline offered its customers as a respite two overnight stays in the capital, Reykjavik, and we took full advantage of the opportunity.

Sandy and I, now seasoned travelers, decided that we had earned a change of pace. After finding a small hotel in the heart of the city, we bedded down the children and set off to enjoy some nightlife. Within a block or so of the hotel, we spotted the inviting lights of a tavern and decided to stop in. We were directed upstairs to the patrons' area where the imbibing was already in full swing. I found a chair and ordered two beers. The waiter, upon hearing the accent, inquired, "Are you Americans?"

I was wary. I'd been hearing about the hostility of Icelanders towards the presence of the US military and also towards the activities of Green Peace, an organization opposed to the whaling industry, which was Iceland's lifeblood. Sandy and I were most pleased and surprised, therefore, when the waiter came back to tell us that a group of older guys wanted the Americans to join them at their table. So we took the opportunity to enjoy some companionship.

The table was occupied by some very seasoned Danish sailors who were well into their 70s. They brought a round of beer—very strong beer—and then another, and yet

218

another. They would not let me reciprocate, which was most acceptable to me. Sandy, a few decades younger than the Danes, was the main attraction for the old guys, and some of the older women at the bar were giving us Americans icy stares.

The seamen were owners of fishing vessels. Friendly as could be. As a matter of fact, too friendly, I was to learn. Sandy sat between two of the old codgers who leaned close to her. The one on her right would tell a story and there'd be ensuing laughter, whereupon the old guy would drape his arm around Sandy's shoulder and let his fingers creep down under her blouse.

"Bill, do you have any idea what is going on, here?" Sandy whispered to me while one of the old guys visited the lavatory. "This guy on my right is reaching down under my blouse every chance he gets."

I was concerned about the codger's behavior, but I also didn't want to stop the beer from flowing. A solution occurred to me. "Why don't you just move closer to the guy on your left," I suggested.

Her response: "Because that one has his hand in my crotch!!"

I moved over next to my wife, and that ended the playfulness on the part of the old guys.

At the time, I had no idea what Green Peace was nor of its action in Icelandic waters to monitor and sometimes halt the whaling. One of the old guys put me on the spot. "And what do you think of Green Peace?" he sneered.

I had no idea how to respond, since I had never heard of the organization. So I blurted out, "They're great with carrots (green peas)." That potentially hostile conversation ended when we were interrupted by a local pilot who joined us at the table.

The young pilot was a most amiable guy, and he told Sandy and me of the many times he had taken Americans up for free rides over the Icelandic countryside in his small plane. "The only thing that bothers me about the Americans is that they never wrote to thank me," he said. I felt badly about that until I tried to get the guy's name and address, and the pilot somehow evaded responding to the request.

Later on I said to Sandy, "No wonder that pilot never got a thank you note. If he wouldn't give someone his address, how could he expect people to write a word of thanks?"

We hired a tour van to take us around the city and to the outlying countryside. Everything was so clean and neat. There was almost no vegetation except low bushes because the climate was too hostile. We were given a tour of a whaling station, where the behemoths were brought in for slaughter. This was done with lances attached to long poles.

Harvard on the Hudson

Once the stomach was sliced open, the most awful smell permeated the huge frame building. It was so bad that we, the onlookers, gagged. It proved to be a most interesting tour, but unfortunately the most lasting memory was the horrible smell.

Iceland was the last leg of our round-the-world adventure. It was now time to fly home and settle back into the lifestyle of upstate New York.

A Memorable Montreal Excursion in the Past

Yet another travel remembrance. While in our early 40's, Sandy and I, together with two other couples with whom we'd been close friends for years, ventured north to Canada to spend a getaway weekend in Montreal. While it promised to be fun, it proved to be doubly so thanks to a suggestion by Fred Hutch, one of the group's fun people.

"I heard about a place we shouldn't miss in Montreal," Fred announced, after we had taken our rooms and unpacked. "It's a night spot called 'La Sex Machine' and I'm told it's like no other place we've ever been."

"I'm not sure I'd enjoy it," Rene Calder commented. None of us was at all surprised. Rene had a reputation for being straight-laced. She'd recently become involved with a fundamentalist religious group, although she never imposed her views on her friends. But Rene had an adventuresome streak, and she didn't wish to prevent the rest of us from having a good time.

As all six of us crammed into the taxi, I heard Peg Hutch icily chide her husband, "Fred, if this proves to be embarrassing, I'll never speak to you again!"

"Where can I take you?" asked the cab driver in his heavy French Canadian accent.

"A bar called La Sex Machine," Fred responded.

"It should be called 'La Rip Off,' the driver wisecracked.

He was fairly close to the mark. There was a minimum charge, and the drinks were astronomically expensive. When it came to amenities, the joint didn't even have a coat rack. And, oh, was it dark and tacky looking.

The lights inside were dim, and there were mirrors on every wall.

"What kind of place is this?" Sandy whispered.

"Unique would seem to describe it," I answered.

As we crossed the carpet on our way to our tables, we descended a few steps between brass posts connected by red velvet rope.

"Classy looking," Peg commented—and then she drew in her breath and exclaimed, "Ack! Take a closer look at those brass posts supporting the red velvet rope!" The brass posts were in the shape of phalluses standing straight and erect with a knob at the top. The design was ingenious. Peg had unfortunately clutched one for support on her way down the steps.

The seating arrangement consisted of horseshoe-shaped booths surrounding glass-topped tables. As we were about to be seated, something unusual caught our attention: the vinyl upholstery on all of the booths throughout the establishment was contoured in the form of naked bosoms. When we sat down, the faux breasts pressed against our backs and our legs. What a sensation!

"Sodom and Gomorrah," Rene remarked.

It was only natural that our next observation would be the glass table around which we all sat. The transparent glass was supported by cleverly designed naked human forms with arms and legs stretched upwards to support the glass tabletop. Some designer had an amazing imagination.

The atmosphere became somewhat tense. While each of us had a good sense of humor, no one was prepared for this.

To break the ice, Renee commented," Is there entertainment?"

Her husband, Bob, interjected, "How much entertainment are you looking for? Did you get a look at the waiter?" That individual was clad only in a loincloth. Rene diverted her eyes only to cast them across the room to see the female bartender, who was topless!

"Well, you've outdone yourself, Fred!" Peg huffed. "There can't be another place as disgusting in the world." She was furious.

There was nowhere anywhere in the entire establishment where you could focus your eyes without seeing something sinful.

"I'm going to just stare at the ceiling," Rene announced, but she followed up that comment with, "Oh my God!"

We all followed her glance toward the ceiling. That was the clincher. It was adorned with foam rubber human parts that continually moved together and apart rhythmically.

"That does it! Time to go! We're out of here!" Peg said, reaching for her coat.

And go we did. To this day we have lasting memories of La Sex Machine. It has sure gotten a lot of mileage when told to friends and family repeatedly over the years. It has even been worth sharing with the grandchildren!

CHAPTER ELEVEN—OFF-CAMPUS LIFE

After returning from that most memorable sabbatical, I resumed my teaching responsibilities at the college. Mark and Grant both left home to enlist in the US Navy for two years.

It was an interesting period in our lives when our two older sons returned from the Navy and were living at home while they attended Hudson College. This required quite an adjustment for both the parents and their sons. Both young men had been living on their own, but to Sandy and me, they were still offspring. It was difficult for the boys to come back to the nest under the protective wing of their parents, and equally as difficult for us parents to accept the independence and maturity of our sons.

The Saga of the M&M's

Mark, 23, might be classified as cerebral: well read, bright, but not very practical.

He owned a car, but his only interest in the vehicle was for transportation. What went on under the hood was of no particular interest to him. When behind the steering wheel, he'd be more likely to be thinking about his passion, sports, rather than driving.

As an aside, Mark was also incredibly forgetful for a young person. He was particularly prone to lock his keys in his car. At the community college, it happened practically on a monthly basis. He became well known to the security force, whom he would contact to unlock the car. When he transferred to Siena, a nearby private college, he locked the keys in his car the very first day of attending class. Off he went to security and informed them of his problem. He ended with the statement, "Please don't forget this face. You're likely to be seeing a lot of me!"

Grant, a year younger than Mark, was also bright, and he was organized and practical as well. He never read more than required. He was very mechanically inclined. To him, driving a car was a challenge, especially in inclement weather. Behind the steering wheel, he was a natural.

A monster snowstorm passed through one Wednesday in February. It swept in at noon and raged on for a day or so. Some fifteen inches of the white stuff came down within twenty-four hours. This was back in the days when I was still driving the Model A Ford Roadster year round. I had left home for the college early in the morning before the snow began to fall heavily. Mark and Grant drove off to the college in separate cars to attend their mid-morning classes.

After the noon hour, Grant had completed his last class for the day and left the campus. At about 3 p.m. Mark appeared at my office.

"I'm going to need some help, Dad," he said. "My car is stuck in the parking lot. I parked pretty close to the Model A."

"Well, I may as well toss in the towel for the day," I thought to myself. The storm isn't letting up, and we'd better be out of here before the roads get too bad."

Without much effort, we freed Mark's car. In attempting to leave the parking space, he had cranked his wheels too much and couldn't get traction until the front wheels were straightened out.

"Mark, now that you're able to move your car, why don't you just wait until I fire up the Model A and then follow me home," I suggested. I'd hate to see you get stuck again." "Good idea," Mark responded, recognizing his own driving limitations.

All went well as we drove out of the college parking lot and onto the main highway. We should have been safely home within a half hour. I attempted to keep track of Mark's car behind me by using my rear view mirror. That worked for a while until the storm increased in intensity. Soon I could barely keep track of the road ahead of me, concentrating more and more on maneuvering the seemingly lighter-than-air Model A. I eventually arrived home, taking much more time than expected.

Sandy, worried about the terrible snowstorm driving conditions, also left her job early and anxiously waited at home for the safe arrival of her brood.

"Where's Mark?" she asked me as I entered the house.

"He should be arriving fairly soon. We had a little trouble getting out of the college parking lot, but he was following me the rest of the way. I lost sight of him about halfway home." I answered.

Minutes passed. Minutes upon minutes upon endless anxious minutes.

"I think you ought to go back and look for Mark," Sandy firmly suggested.

"You've got to be kidding," I responded with disbelief. "Mark is a grown man. He's driving a much more reliable car than mine. I'll be damned if I'm going back out there in this weather. Let's just wait a little longer. I'm sure he'll be home shortly."

More minutes passed. Finally the phone rang. It was Mark.

"Dad, I slid off the road and went into a ditch. Don't worry about me. Both the car and I are in good shape. I'll get home somehow."

I passed the news on to Sandy, who promptly went into orbit. "You've got to go after him. Right now! He could be lying in the road freezing to death! Or he could be in some terrible accident!"

I reasoned, "Now hold on a minute. He just phoned from someone's house. They don't have phones in ditches. He'll be fine. He said so."

Luckily, Grant arrived at that moment, cheerfully stomping snow off his feet and onto the living room rug.

"Where have you been in this weather?" His mother demanded to know.

Grant's answer was unbelievable: "I thought it might be fun to drive down to the homestead just to see how pretty it looked in the snow!"

"Yeah, right," I thought. "I'll bet you made some doughnuts by driving in circles in the cornfield just to see if that shitcan of a car of yours would take the punishment." Needless to say, I didn't share that particular thought with Sandy.

She peered out the window. Grant's vehicle was nowhere in sight. Instead, his Uncle Larry's blue pickup truck, which had been garaged at the homestead while Larry was at sea with the merchant marines, was now parked out front.

"What are you doing with your uncle's truck?" Sandy asked.

"I got my car stuck on the dirt road leading into the homestead," Grant confessed, looking at the floor in embarrassment.

"But why did you drive way down there in the first place?" his mother questioned.

There was a lengthy pause before Grant answered, "I guess I don't know. I just wanted to do it."

"The hell you don't know," I thought. "I've known you long enough to realize you just couldn't wait to get out there and battle the elements. It wasn't that long ago that I had such inspirations myself."

Harvard on the Hudson

"Grant, how about joining me in a search for your brother?" I suggested. "He phoned home about an hour ago. He said the car was in a ditch, so I guess we should go look for him. Since you have the truck and it has good snow tires and a towrope, we should be in good shape.

"I'm ready when you are. Let's hit the road." Grant's enthusiasm truly annoyed Sandy.

Once in the truck, I pressed Grant for more information. "Is there something more you'd like to tell me? Like what compelled you to drive to the homestead. There seems to be a piece of the puzzle missing."

"You know how it is, Dad," he confessed. "Weather like this gets my adrenalin pumping. I couldn't wait to see how my car would handle in a heavy snowstorm. When I got to the homestead, I practiced a few doughnuts in the cornfield and then drove down and around the dump just to see if I could make it. On the way back home from the homestead, I ran my car off the road and had to walk back to get Uncle Larry's truck. I'm sure he wouldn't mind my using it under the circumstances." At last the full story had come out.

I continued, "I'm sure he wouldn't mind either. But let's get back to what was going on inside of your head as you drove off for several miles into the country on such a shitty day. Surely you could have horsed around closer to home."

"I'm going to tell you the truth, Dad. Do you think you can handle it," Grant leveled.

"I can deal with it. It's been such a weird day that nothing else could surprise me. Try me," I urged.

Grant explained, "I drove down there because I somehow remembered that I had a big bag of M&M's in my jacket at the homestead. I thought it would be great to have some M&M's on a day like today."

I just shook my head. "Promise me this will never get to your mother's ears, Grant," I commented.

We never did find Mark or his car in spite of tracing and retracing the route to and from the college. Eventually we gave up. That's when Mark drove his car into the driveway. Apparently he'd gotten himself a tow job.

"Where have you guys been all this time?" Mark asked.

"Let's talk about it later," I suggested, heading toward the bedroom for a much-needed nap.

"M&M's!"   I repeated over and over to myself as I dozed off.

Getting Them Up and Off to School

There was a period of time when Sandy was scheduled to go to work at daybreak, and I was delegated the onerous task of getting the children off to school before my own classes started at the college. This was a particularly harrowing experience because (a) not all of the children liked getting up in the morning,   (b) not all of the children liked going to school, and (c) not all of the children liked sharing the family's one and only bathroom. I dreaded the responsibility, but there was no choice.

One memorable February morning, I awoke to the 6 a.m. alarm. Time to get them up and on their way. The school bus stopped at 8 a.m., and before that each of the five siblings living at home was allocated twenty minutes—and not a minute more—in the john. Jennifer was the first up. Groggily she staggered into the bathroom.

"This is going to take a long time; I can sense it," I thought to myself, listening to the endless running of the shower and later the whirr of the hair dryer. Forty-five minutes later, the princess stepped out of the bathroom.

"One down, four to go. I'm glad the older boys are in the Navy," I thought. "I could never have gotten all seven out of the house on time."

"Giss, your turn in the john," I called across the upstairs hall.

"I don't feel well. My head hurts. I think I'll stay home and rest," Giss announced.

The hell you will," I stormed. "You've missed too much school already this year. I'll give you half an hour more to rest, and then it's up and out of here."

"Heather, you're next. You'll have to take Giss' turn in the lineup. Giss will follow after you," I directed.

"I won't be going in to school until nine o'clock so I'm in no hurry to get ready." Heather said.

"Nine o'clock? Is that something special just for today?" I asked.

"Oh, no," Heather replied, "that's for the rest of the year."

"How come?" I pressed. "You've always had an eight-thirty class. Has your schedule been changed?"

"No," Heather explained. "My first class is math. I decided I don't like it, so I'm not going anymore."

I could feel my blood pressure rising. "Not going anymore? Just like that? You don't like something and so you're just going to avoid it? Get out of that bed and get your butt in gear."

By now an hour had passed. I could see the entire schedule falling to pieces. There was only one thing to do — cool off for a few minutes, but in the meantime buy valuable time by getting son Greg into the bathroom.

Greg, by his preference, had taken up residence in the basement, two stories down. It had once been a bare

room, but we'd done it over to make a kid's hangout—
black walls, fluorescent stars on the ceiling, water bed—
the works.

The best way for me to communicate with the boy from
my bedroom on the second floor was to get down on my
hands and knees and shout down through the forced-air
duct. To make matters worse, Greg was by far the hardest
one to awaken. The boy simply hated getting up in the
morning.

"Greg!" I shouted down through the register.

No response.

"Greg, get up. You're next in the bathroom. Get up now
or you'll be late for school."

A grunt came up from far below in the bowels of the
basement.

"Damn it, Greg, get up or I'll come down there and pull
you out of bed. "Finally, a sleepy response, "I don't have to
go in for the rest of the week, Dad."

It was a response, all right, but not the one I wanted to
hear. Losing the last measure of patience, I shouted down
through the air duct, "What do you mean you don't have
to go in for the rest of the week? What in hell is going
on?" I was close to being apoplectic.

"Don't fly off the handle, Dad," he responded calmly. "There's nothing to get upset about. I've been suspended."

With that, I gave up the fight. I dressed, picked up my valise, walked out of the house, quietly closed the door behind me, and drove off to college in the car.

"It's only eight in the morning and already the day has turned to shit," I muttered, backing out of the driveway. "I'd better get away from this place before I kill all of them!"

How the Dog Spent Christmas Eve

The day before Christmas was one of the most bitterly cold in history. There was a crust on the six inches of snow, and the winds were ferocious. Not a nice day to be out of doors.

Ozzie, the black lab family pet, and I were never friends. I never considered myself a "dog person," although many memorable and personable canines had found their way into the family when the children were young. Sandy loved dogs. Ozzie was friendly but she was also very stupid and she had the worst case of body odor imaginable. Sandy would become very defensive when I criticized the dog.

"She smells terrible," I'd often say. You give her baths time and time again, yet every time I touch her, my hands absolutely stink. What's wrong with the damned dog—and why do we keep her?"

"She can't help it." Sandy explained. Her skin contains rare oils. All labs have the same problem."

I put up with it. I'd even loosened up and taken the dog along for an outing at the family homestead in the country. There were forty acres over which the dog could roam. She loved getting out of doors after so many cold winter days cooped up in the house.

And so it was on that bitterly cold day before Christmas. Ozzie eagerly bounded into the front seat of the pickup truck, eyeing me with total adoration as we drove the ten-mile distance.

"Why do you look at me with such loving eyes?" I said to her. "I'm not at all fond of you because you do stupid things and you smell something awful."

Ozzie just licked her chops and continued her affectionate stare.

When we arrived, the dog jumped down from the truck, off for a few hours of afternoon exercise in spite of the frigid temperatures. I had my own agenda: chopping wood, taking a walk, and just enjoying the quietness of a vacation day during the college's holiday break.

This was living.

When late afternoon arrived and the shadows began to fall, I had my usual late afternoon cup of tea and then drove back to the city. After dinner, I would be taking the older children to the Christmas Eve service at church.

The bitter cold weather worsened as darkness settled in. The temperatures dropped to ten degrees below zero, and the wind chill made it seem much worse.

After the church service at 9 p.m., I returned home with the older children. Standing in the doorway to greet us, hands on hips, was Sandy.

"Where's the dog?" she asked.

"Isn't she here?" I responded.

"No, she's not here. You didn't bring her into the house when you got back from the homestead. Where is she?"

Famous for my forgetfulness, I strived to maintain composure. "I must have left her out in the country. No problem. I'll drive down and pick her up first thing in the morning!"

"Bill, that dog will freeze to death out in the cold on a night like tonight," Sandy fumed. "You'd better get back into the truck and get down there to get her—*Right Now!*" Relief from the intensifying drama arrived in the form of son Mark, who had just pulled into the driveway. "Mark, how about doing me a real favor?" I asked. "Apparently, I left the damned dog down at the homestead. Would you please drive down and get her for me?"

Mark wasn't at all enthusiastic about the idea, and I knew exactly why. Even at the ripe age of nineteen, the boy was terrified of the homestead at night. It was miles from anywhere. It was dark. The house was locked. There was even a family cemetery at the top of the hill. And then, to add to the mix, there were those numerous frightening ghost stories he'd heard from Dad repeatedly over the years.

"Do I have to go, Dad?"

"I'd really appreciate it, Mark. Your mother and I have a lot to get done preparing for Christmas Day before hitting the sack."

By the time Mark drove to the homestead it was nearing eleven at night. He was shaking with fear. The only lights to be seen were on the outdoor Christmas trees his uncle had decorated for the season. Other than that, there was total darkness, howling wind, and the biting cold. He could see the outline of the old stone house looming in the night—and even a few of the tombstones up on the hill.

With a quavering voice, Mark called for the dog—over and over again. No sign of her. Mark was so hoping Ozzie would appear, but it was not to be. So he set out to walk the premises to find the dog. Every wind gust and every rustling branch made him freeze with fear. He decided to stay within the area of the lighted Christmas tree, until suddenly the lights went off when the timer switch activated. He froze in his tracks.

The last thing he wanted to do was go into the foreboding house, but he had to use the phone to call home. There were no cell phones back then. He found the key, opened the door, and made his way inside. He cursed the lack of central heating.

"Dad, I can't find the dog," his voice quavered. "I called and called. She's nowhere to be found."

"Thanks for trying, Mark. You'd better give up the search and come back home." Words Mark was so anxious to hear.

I met Mark out on the porch, deliberately out of earshot of Sandy. While Mark was pouring out his terrorized tale of the search, there came the sound of muffled barking, breaking through the night air. It was coming from inside the cap of the pickup truck.

"Oh my God! It's the damned dog!" I exclaimed. "I must have put her in the back of the pickup truck, and she's been in there all this time. How did I ever forget about her?"

When I released the tailgate, a very cold but very happy adoring dog jumped to the ground. She didn't even know enough to be pissed off about being cooped up in frigid temperatures for so long. I couldn't wait to present Sandy with the great news: the dog had been found!

Was she pleased? Not at all.

"Do you mean to tell me that you left that dog in the truck for eight hours in below zero temperatures?" she snarled. "What is going on in your head?"

I closed the conversation with the meek observation that at least the dog had been at the church for Christmas Eve services. Sandy wasn't at all amused.

Driving Clunkers

<u>The VW van that wouldn't stop:</u>

Driving tired, old, rusty, used cars was a way of life for my wife and me. She hated it; I saw it more as a challenge. I reasoned that it was a way to economize when raising a family of seven children. Some of the vehicles were especially memorable, such as the 1968 VW van I bought in the late 1970s. This vehicle ended its career with the family because it was too costly to maintain.

The problem was that VW's needed to be maintained by VW dealers, and that's where the heavy expenses were incurred. There had to be some irony in the coincidence that each visit to the shop seemed to involve almost exactly a $200 outlay—a pretty hefty sum at that time. It didn't seem to matter what the problem was; the solution invariably involved forking over $200.

Visit number one was for brakes: parts—$89, labor—$111, total—$200. Next came the tune-up: parts—$28, labor—$172, total—$200. Visit number three (within three months of visits one and two) was to have the tie rod replaced to correct steering and tire-wearing problems: parts—$59, labor—$141, total—$200. Uncanny! Not long thereafter, exhaust system problems developed. As I approached the service manager, I thought, "Why don't I just write this guy a check for $200 and let him allocate the parts and labor?" Guess what the exhaust system repair cost: $200!

The final straw was the transmission problem.

At the time, we lived in a two-story brick home located on a side street in the city of Rensselaer, New York. The house was just one block off the main thoroughfare, Washington Avenue, and could be accessed by just driving around the block. Across the street from us lived Bill Reimann (Sandy's brother) and his wife, Laura. Some three or four miles away was the VW dealership.

It was a warm summer evening when I parked the van to attend a meeting in the lower end of the town. Back home, Sandy had opened the windows to enjoy some night air while watching TV and reclining on the living room sofa.

I had noticed transmission problems soon after I got into the van. I had trouble shifting into first gear. Disengaging the clutch was difficult. It became increasingly difficult to shift gears each time I goosed the engine after stopping for a traffic light. I sensed that before the evening was over, I would have to make the choice of either stopping the van and leaving it where it was or leaving it in gear and simply keep moving along. With the clutch out of commission, there was no hope of starting the vehicle once it was in gear.

The choice was suddenly thrust upon me as I was returning home from the meeting. Several blocks from home, the van absolutely refused to shift out of first gear.

"Somehow I've got to get the damned thing to the VW dealer," I reasoned, "but it's getting late at night and they are closed. I'll just have to leave it in their parking lot and call in the morning. There aren't any phones out that way (this in the days long before cell phones), so I'll have to tell Sandy to have her brother meet me at the VW place and drive me back home. But how can I tell Sandy if I can't stop the damned car at the house? I'll just have to keep it moving forward, or it will jam in gear.

I decided to take a chance and cruise slowly past the house while trying to get Sandy's attention by shouting to her from the van as I drove by. Creeping along, I approached the house. "Sandy!" I yelled out the van window. I had no way of knowing if she heard my call because I had to cruise on around the block. I approached the house on the second lap. "Sandy!" I called out again, and cruised on around the block a second time.

By the second pass, Sandy knew something very strange was going on. She would hear someone familiar call out her name, but by the time she got to the door, there was no one in sight. It happened a third time. On the fourth cycle, she waited in the doorway.

Along came the VW van. Spotting my wife, I called out, "Tell your brother..." That's all I could manage before the van was too far on its way for me to be heard.

I made yet another round. On the fifth pass, hoping she remembered my first message, I added, "to meet me at the VW dealer..." and onward I cruised.

On the sixth pass I finished up with, "as soon as he can get there!"

On my seventh and final pass, I yelled to Sandy, "I can't stop this goddamned thing!" Off I drove to the VW dealership. Sandy contacted her brother, and the plan was followed.

The full cost of the transmission job was: $200. Shortly thereafter, an ad appeared in the classified section of the newspaper. "Cozy VW van for sale," it read. We'd had it with that damned van and its endless thirst for costly repairs.

A few days later, a young hippie couple appeared on the doorstep. After some discussion, I confessed that the van had experienced several mechanical problems. This didn't seem to bother the potential buyers in the least.

"We're more interested in having the van to live in, rather than for transportation," the guy said. Sounded like a genuine hippie to me.

"Then this is just the car for you!" I declared, as he accepted the cash price for the VW van: $200!

Blissfully, the young couple drove off in the van of their dreams.

The self-propelled mystery car

Sandy once had a car which caused her considerable distress. She claimed that after she had turned the key off and gone into the house, it would start up and move down the street by itself. I just couldn't believe it, and I told her so. Rather than get into an altercation about the alleged problem, I suggested she phone our dependable garage man, Al Martino, a terrific mechanic. About 70 years old or so, he was also patient, understanding, and soft spoken. One of the nicest guys I'd ever known.

Sandy phoned him, and I eavesdropped on the conversation (as she suggested) using the upstairs phone.

"Al, I have a problem with my car," Sandy said.

"Tell me what's giving you trouble, Mrs. Stevens." Al replied.

"Well, Al, sometimes when I leave the car out in front of the house, it starts up by itself," Sandy explained.

There was a thoughtful pause at the other end of the line. Then Al said, "You say it starts up all by itself?"

"Yes, Al, all by itself—without me in it."

Another thoughtful pause. "I guess I never heard of that before, Mrs. Stevens," Al said. "You say it starts up all by itself. That's interesting. Then what does it do?"
"Sometimes it backs down the street. All by itself," Sandy replied.

I could hear Al tsk-tsking at the other end of the line. "You say it backs down the street all by itself?" he repeated. "Boy, that's a new one on me."

I could tell that the guy was trying to be polite, but that he agreed with me that her concern was pure fantasy.

"Why don't you bring it in and let me take a look at it," Al suggested. "Boy, I never heard of that one," he muttered as he put down the phone. I could just picture the old guy shaking his head in disbelief.

I have no idea what Al did, but he did something—enough to calm Sandy's concern. Shortly after that, Sandy bought another car.

The Money Maker

The Chevy station wagon, vintage 1951, was another real gem. I paid $600 for it and had it two years. I bought it in the mid 1970s. Light blue with rust.

Delighted with the bargain, I burst into the house and proudly announced to Sandy, "I just bought another car." Prior to this, we had owned a series of lemons, and she was not happy about it.

"And just what color and rust is it?" was her sarcastic response.

We drove it all over. I can remember the time we took all seven kids up to Canton in upstate New York to visit her sister. When it came time to depart, several of her sister's family had to push it out of the yard to get it started.

The station wagon was continuously in and out of the garage for repairs. At the time we had another great mechanic, Mike, who had a serious stuttering problem. Like Al, he was a great guy, patient and sympathetic. We never had to wait for him to tackle a repair problem. I guess you would say that we were preferred customers.

After two years or so, the car died while I was shopping at a store right across the street from Mike's garage.

He immediately walked across the street to my rescue. After a few routine tests, he looked at me and announced, "W-w-well, th-th-there g-goes the m-m-m-moneymaker." Time for another clunker.

<u>More car problems</u>

When the children were very young in the early '60s, we rented the north wing of the homestead which my older brother owned. At only $25 a month, it was a bargain, but it was pure country living and a real hardship for Sandy. At that time, she had a part-time job waiting tables and was scheduled to work irregular hours, usually in the evening, but once in a while in the morning. I would babysit if she worked the evening shift, but if she were called in for the morning shift, I would have to drive the little ones (we had two at the time) to my Mom's for babysitting while I performed my teaching obligations at

Hudson High School some thirty miles away. It was a hectic schedule, but we managed for a few years.

In those days, I did almost all of my car repairs. On my salary, it was one sure way to cut down on expenses.

The rusty gas tank

Some of the clunkers were really memorable in an agonizing way. We once owned an old beat-up Nash that was only with us a few months. There was that night when Sandy worked until 11 p.m. It was raining, and the river had just about reached flood stage. The access road to the homestead was partially under water, and so the only safe way to get in to the house was to drive down the shoulder of the railroad, which was some ten feet in elevation and protected from flooding.

Picture the scene: poor Sandy was tired; it was raining; it was the dark of night; and yes, she was several months pregnant. It was a "perfect storm" of negative circumstances. That's precisely when the gas tank decided to break through its rusty supports and fall onto the railroad bed. Sandy simply abandoned the car and trudged through the rain to get back to the family.

The loose lug nut

Some months later, I had to repair a flat tire on the damned car. I neglected to tighten the lugs that held the wheels on the car. Subsequently, when Sandy was driving the car to work, the vehicle suddenly lurched and then dropped down to the road on one side. The wheel had come off! Boy, did I get in trouble over that!

The blanket fiasco

The Nash had a very tired battery. On very cold mornings, it was tough to get it started. The motor would turn over a few times and then grind to a sickening halt. I'd learned sometime earlier that it helped to put a blanket over the engine before the engine cooled down at night and then firmly close the hood to keep out the cold. I had an old, heavy-duty army blanket that was just right for the job.

One wintery week, we had a particularly severe cold spell. For a few nights running, I applied the old blanket-over-engine trick and it worked out successfully.
Then came the morning when I neglected to open the hood and remove the blanket before starting up the car. In spite of my oversight, it started up and ran well.

I gathered up young Mark and Grant, loaded them into the back seat of the Nash, and then began the drive toward the city where they would be dropped off at my mother's.

Harvard on the Hudson

After driving a few miles north on Route 9J, I distinctly smelled smoke. Then I saw smoke seeping out of the hood. And then the seeping smoke became a billowing cloud. It still hadn't occurred to me that the blanket was still covering the motor, which had heated up to the danger point. I pulled the car to a stop on the country highway and immediately carried the boys to a safe distance away. Then I went back to the car and opened the hood. All of that oxygen rushed in, and the blanket burst into flames.

Of course there appeared an audience of other car drivers. Talk about being embarrassed! The others were on their way to work, and I was holding them up. One woman gathered up the boys and put them in her car where it was warm.

The fire was quite a sight to behold. It burned every bit of combustible material in the engine: wire insulation, hoses, etc.—every bit. At that point, the Nash was history. I had it towed off to the nearest junk yard and began the search for yet another clunker.

Photographing the State Capitols—Every Damned One of the Fifty

It wasn't an intentional goal at first, but eventually I photographed each of the fifty state capitol buildings in the USA. The process took me approximately fifty years.

It all started on our honeymoon back in the summer of 1957. I always had a camera on hand, and our honeymoon travels through New England started off the adventure. Concord, New Hampshire, and Augusta, Maine, were the initial inductees into the photo collection.

At later dates in our marriage, Sandy and I visited Boston and Providence, and I added two more domed buildings to the collection. Then there was a semester of weekend courses at the University of Connecticut for me, and thus the gold-domed capitol at Hartford complemented the budding collection.

Naturally, Albany, New York, our home stomping ground, provided one more photo op as did those at nearby Trenton, New Jersey, and Harrisburg, Pennsylvania. In all of this time, it never occurred to me that I was on a roll.

Harvard on the Hudson

On our way to Australia in 1965, I was sure to photograph King Kamehameha's palace in Honolulu, Hawaii, which at the time was the capitol building. That building is no longer the capitol because a much more modern structure has since taken its place. Sandy and I were able to incorporate the more modern building into the photo collection when taking our post-retirement trip.

The other distant capitol was in Juneau, Alaska, a simple structure that seemed disappointingly similar to an unadorned grade school I had attended in my youth during the 1930s.

We were able to do that while on a 10-day trip that consisted of flying to Fairbanks, taking the train to Denali and then on to Anchorage, flying to Juneau, and completing the trip by taking the ferry down the inland waterway to Bellingham, Washington.

These capitol visitations began to wear thin with Sandy. After forty or so, she rebelled. "I have no intention of driving into the center of a city just so you can take a picture of a damned building," she snarled as we proceeded on a Midwest sojourn.

One of the breaking points occurred in downtown Columbus, Ohio. Sandy was driving through a tightly congested swarm of people getting out of work at 5 p.m. It was uncomfortably hot and humid, and her mood was downright surly.

"Stop here," I gently suggested as the capitol came into view.

"I'll be damned if I'll stop here or anywhere else in this traffic just so you can take a picture of a stupid building!" she exclaimed.

When the car stopped for a red light, I opened the door to get out.

"If you get out, you're not getting back in," my wife threatened.

"That's OK with me," I retorted, "but just remember: I have the wallet and credit cards with me."

After I had taken the picture, I got back into a very quiet car. The silence lasted for several hours.

The other explosion occurred when I lied to Sandy about the route we were to take in Wisconsin. I told her we were on our way to the upper Michigan peninsula, and we were, except we were taking a circuitous route that involved a detour of about 100 miles. The capitol building at Madison was glorious—in my opinion. To Sandy, it was an unnecessary diversion that had caused her an extra two hours of driving. She was livid!

In the final segment of my quest to photo capitol buildings—by now it had become an obsession—I decided to wing it on a solo drive through the plains states and beyond, including Kansas, Missouri, Nebraska, Iowa, the Dakotas, Wyoming, Colorado, New Mexico, Oklahoma, and Arkansas. It was a fun trip that provided me with opportunities to visit a number of friends who had settled far from New York State.

The most frustrating segment of the journey occurred on the way to Little Rock, Arkansas. Along the way, the interstate began to be divided by an endless succession of concrete barriers set up during a vast construction project. Hard to believe, but the damned, intimidating obstacles were continuous for more than fifty miles. Needless to say, on my return trip from photographing the capitol, I followed less-traveled highways.

The last of the state capitols to be photographed was in Salem, Oregon. Sandy and I were to enjoy a ten-day trip along the Oregon coast. Rather than inflict yet another capitol on Sandy, I surreptitiously sneaked out of our motel on the coastal highway at 4 a.m. and drove some 80 miles inland to capture on film the 50th and final state capitol for the collection.

It took some time to develop a photo album of the fifty state capitols, but eventually that task was completed.

In my opinion, the white vertical tower at Baton Rouge, Louisiana, is the most attractive capitol building, followed by a similar grey tower in Lincoln, Nebraska. Juneau's is the homeliest. Albany, New York's, capitol is of French chateau style and would have been so much more impressive if sliding soil conditions hadn't prevented a dome from being constructed in the center. The most "far-out" is the very modern circular atrocity in New Mexico. To me, it looked more like a glorified fuel storage tank. Many of the capitols were almost repetitive in appearance, including Cheyenne, Wyoming; Lansing, Michigan; Springfield, Illinois; and Indianapolis, Indiana.

It was on the trip to Seattle, Washington, that we had the most serious problem with luggage that we ever encountered in all of our many travels. We had flown to Seattle and had taken a shuttle bus directly to the car rental agency. When I reached to take our luggage out of the bus and into the car rental kiosk, an ambitious attendant took the luggage away before I could get it. "It's my job, sir," he smiled.

At the time, this irked me slightly because so many pieces of luggage looked alike—same color, size, and shape—and I was afraid we might not get our own luggage in the process.

Harvard on the Hudson

That's exactly what happened!

Unfortunately, I momentarily abandoned my concerns and proceeded to go through the process of renting the car.

That night in Astoria, Oregon, some 150 miles south of Seattle, Sandy opened what she assumed to be her luggage when we arrived at the motel. Now you must understand that at this stage of her life, Sandy had put on some weight and was comfortably "wholesome" in stature. So it was with considerable dismay that in the suitcase were a spaghetti-strap bra, lacey mini-panties, spiked heels, and other paraphernalia suited to a much younger and slimmer woman. At first we were awe struck, and then the humor of our predicament kicked in. We were scheduled for a ten-day vacation, and this was to be her wardrobe—NOT! We also sympathized with the dear young thing who opened her suitcase and found Sandy's attire inside. The next day, we made a brief stopover at Wal-Mart to buy more suitable clothing.

It was more than a week later when we returned to the kiosk in Seattle to get back our own luggage. We often wondered how our counterpart survived the ordeal.

W. L. Staats

Some Interesting Personalities

Timothy—The Visitor Who Wouldn't Go Away

Warning: This vignette is grim!

With the family homestead located on the east shore of the Hudson River, the elements—tides, currents, floods, floating debris—make life interesting. Dead bodies are always a dreaded concern, particularly the thought of bumping into one while boating or swimming. I was spared the anguish of seeing one until I was well into my forties.

The first corpse, later identified as Mr. Romano, was an octogenarian who had been in the water for several months over the winter. He had washed up on the shore just a few hundred feet above our property.

"Kids, I have something macabre to show you that I'll bet you've never seen before," I announced to the three eldest offspring one spring afternoon. There in the weeds along the river shore was an outstretched leg—more accurately a leg bone with a sneaker on the bony foot. The skull was almost skinless. The body was fully clothed. It certainly impressed the children, and it particularly impressed me, too, when the coroner jammed his rubber-gloved finger into the fellow's mouth, checking for identifying teeth.

Harvard on the Hudson

The experience was horrifying and unforgettable. I could have spared the youngsters the trauma, but I felt they could benefit by the experience and perhaps be better prepared to handle something similar in the future.

The Romano "discovery" happened early in the '70s. Some ten years passed before Timothy—who arrived on the scene and wouldn't leave it—was found.

It was a warm Sunday evening. The majority of the family had left the homestead after dinner. As the sun was setting, a New York State Trooper drove into the yard. The young officer ambled over to me as I was seated on the veranda enjoying the last fleeting minutes of daylight.

"One of your neighbors across the river phoned us, he said. They think they spotted a body on the shore about a mile north of here. Since there are no roads leading into that area, I was wondering if you would mind taking me for a boat ride up to see what's there."

I shuddered.

"I'll be only too happy to accommodate you, officer," I volunteered. "All I have is a thirteen-foot aluminum boat with a six-horsepower outboard motor."

"It never hurts to help out the State Police," I reminded myself.

Within minutes we were on our way, scanning the east shoreline as we cruised north. The trooper related to me that a young inmate from the Capital District Psychiatric Center had wandered away. His name was Timothy. A few days later, he'd been seen standing on the Dunn Memorial Bridge, which spans the Hudson between Albany and Rensselaer. Someone had reported seeing a young man jump over the bridge railing.

Just as darkness closed in, we made the grim discovery. A human corpse was lying on a secluded beach.

"That's him right there face down on the beach," the trooper said. We pulled the boat onto the sandy beach near Timothy's body. Timothy was a frightening sight. His skin was the color of chalk. He was fully clothed, and there were not yet signs of decomposition.

"I've never seen the body of someone young before. What a gruesome sight," I silently mused.

It surely was gruesome. Timothy's head was turned to one side. Something, perhaps a seagull or fish, had eaten away his left eye.

The trooper politely ordered me, "You'll have to go back home and telephone (cell phones were not yet prevalent) for help from the Castleton Rescue Squad. Make sure they send an ambulance up to your property. I have to stay here with the body."

"Why?" I asked.

"It's the rules," the officer replied.

"What if it just so happened that we discovered the body floating down the river? Would you still have to stay with him?" I asked.

"I guess not," the officer responded, "but that isn't the situation, is it?"

"Can't we just load him into the boat or maybe tie a rope to his leg and pull him along behind?" I persisted.

"You certainly have a weird sense of humor, Mr. Stevens, he replied. " Now why don't you just get into your boat and go home and make the phone call?"

I obeyed. One always obeys the police.

It was nighttime when the Castleton Rescue Squad appeared with a boat. Northward they cruised up the river to meet with the trooper. An hour later, the group arrived with its eerie cargo at the beach area at the homestead. Timothy lay in a metal-framed body basket. He was deposited onto the rocky beach.

Not long afterward, the Castleton ambulance arrived with a crew of enthusiastic volunteers. Radio contact was made with the Capital District Psychiatric Center to confirm Timothy's identity. In the darkness, flashlights were used to scan the corpse. Hushed voices whispered in the dark, giving directions, answering questions, and planning the next step in the process.

Timothy, arms folded across his stomach, was carted up from the shore and deposited on the lawn. All was going smoothly, and then a glitch interrupted the plan.

A serious jurisdictional dispute arose when it came to determining who would pay for the ambulance. The Psychiatric Center refused to pay since Timothy was not found on their premises. The city of Albany and the Albany county authorities were contacted, since Timothy had leaped from the bridge on the Albany side of the river. They refused to pay because Timothy's body had been found on the Rensselaer county shore of the Hudson. Of course the Rensselaer county authorities refused payment on the basis that Timothy was not a county resident. The Castleton Ambulance refused to move Timothy until the matter of payment was settled. All of this wrangling was done by radio and phone and was clearly audible to me and my family.

As the arguing went on, Timothy's corpse just lay there in the body basket facing the stars.

Toward midnight, the matter had still not been resolved. I felt a touch of humor was needed, and so I approached the young trooper.

"Why don't you just leave Timothy here with us for the rest of the summer," I facetiously suggested. "We could prop him up in a comfortable rocking chair on the verandah and place a martini in his hand. It sure would make a conversation piece for visitors."

"Mr. Stevens, you have strange sense of humor," the irritated officer replied. "Would you mind going to bed—right now?"

I obeyed. One always obeys the police.

By the next morning, Timothy had departed the scene, ambulance, body basket, and all.

The Larsens

Sandy and I had a knack of making friends for life. Once we had cemented a relationship, we clung to it tenaciously even well after we ceased to have much in common. It worked for several decades with high school classmates, college friends, teaching colleagues, and ever so many friends who came into the picture through family contact.

And so it was with the Larsens.

Directly across the Hudson River from the homestead was a lovely old wood- frame house occupied by a fine family we never met until Mark and Grant and I were in Melbourne, Australia, in the late '70s. Sandy had a close friend who did volunteer work at the Albany Medical Center. This friend was also close with another volunteer worker, Mrs. Anita Larsen from across the river.

Sandy wrote to inform me that Paul Larsen, Anita's husband, was temporarily assigned to the job of locating a prospective factory site for an Albany-area woolen mill to be located in Australia. Paul had investigated locations near Sydney and Adelaide where the transportation and labor supply were suitable, but he liked the Melbourne area even better. He rented a place near Geelong, some thirty miles southwest of Melbourne. I phoned Paul, and he was delighted to hear from a neighbor from across his beloved Hudson River.

We met for lunch, and we struck up a mutual admiration friendship even though Paul was some twenty years or so my senior. Later on, Anita flew over, and while she was in the Melbourne, the Larsen's treated me to a lavish dinner at one of the city's finest hotels. What a great evening we had. That was the start of a friendship that lasted for decades.

Harvard on the Hudson

While at the homestead in the summer during the 80s, we would see the Larsens on the beach across the river. Through binoculars we could see that they knew how to enjoy themselves. They would carry down portable reclining lounges and stretch out in the sun for hours. Apparently sipping bourbon was part of the routine.

Now and then they would get carried away and lie contentedly until the tide came up to their beach recliners. One time Anita became immobile, and we saw Paul literally dragging her by the arm to get away from the rising waters. It was like that scene from the movie "Rear Window" where Jimmy Stewart witnesses a suspected murder from his apartment window. This scene, however, had no such dire implications, but it convinced Sandy and me that the Larsens knew how to relax!

Over the years, we would often visit. I would row over and spend a few hours with them on the beach, and they would return the favor by rowing over to attend social outings with us and our family and friends. They were wonderful people, well off but down to earth. In cooler weather, they would host truly delightful parties with their upscale friends: bank presidents, industrial executives, volunteers belonging to auxiliary groups, etc. Fine people. It was a privilege for a run-of-the-mill college teacher to mingle with such a refined group.

Some of the parties were doozies. Booze was always flowing, and the fun times included an elderly couple singing a well-practiced duet as well as so many jokes, puns, and stories. One elegant lady suggested that we all should try her favorite pastime: crawling under the Christmas tree with a martini and gazing up at the lights while lying flat on her back. "Try it; you'll love it!" she urged. And we did.

One summer party put on at the home of friends from nearby Delmar was most memorable. They had a large deck out back that was accessed by sliding aside a screen door. Out on the deck there was a display of booze. Paul Larsen and I were having a jovial time, and he decided to meander out on the deck for just another sip. Unfortunately, he forgot about the sliding screen door, and he walked right into it. The door came off its hinges, and Paul fell forward, door and all, onto the deck. The hosts apologized, insisting that the screen door had problems and they had meant to tell us about it. Anita was dismayed by the incident, but Paul wasn't seriously injured, and the sliding screen door was put back in place. We resumed making merry.

Minutes later, I decided to have a refill. Hard to believe, but I forgot about the damned door and did exactly the same thing as Paul. I walked into the door, it let go at the hinges, and I fell flat on my face. This time the hosts were equally apologetic, but I could sense the tension when I stood up and looked at Sandy. She was livid.

When we got home, I received the expected tongue-lashing: how I should take better control of myself — how thoughtless I was — how embarrassing for her — and on and on and on. What defense could I give? I was guilty as charged.

The next day I rowed across to apologize for my indiscretion. Paul assured me that there was no big problem and that the whole matter should be forgotten. I was so grateful that I had not disgraced myself.

When I got home, I confronted Sandy. "It really wasn't fair of you to reprimand me for last night's behavior," I maintained. "I talked with Paul Larsen, and he said there was no big problem worth remembering."

"Paul Larsen!" Sandy retorted. "Why would you listen to Paul Larsen? He was drunker than you were!" The rest of the day was quiet.

We maintained our close friendship with our older neighbors from across the river. We accompanied them on a grand trip to Montreal for a weekend, and at a later date, we stayed with them at the historic Grafton Inn north of Brattleboro, Vermont. They were a fun couple to be with.

I recall something Anita said when she attended daughter Giss's wedding. I was introducing her to my new son-in-law, and she remarked, concerning Sandy and me, "Do you know they spy on us from across the river?" I felt guilty about the accusation but had to admit it was true. Our binoculars enabled us to keep an eye on them.

Later on in the summer, however, I was visiting their home and when entering their living room, I noted a professionally mounted telescope trained in the direction of our home across the river. It was so powerful that I could see the color of the croquet balls on our lawn. So much for us spying on them!!

The years passed too quickly. By the '90s, Paul had developed Parkinson's disease, and not long after he had to go to a nursing home. Anita visited him every day and I would try to stop by to see him on a bi-weekly basis. It is such a sad disease. Paul's mind was still very acute, but he had no locomotion skills. Eventually, he couldn't even manage the TV remote. Mercifully, he passed way after a few years.

His two older daughters had a most unusual request. "Father wished to be cremated and have his ashes scattered in the Hudson. He loved the river so," his daughter Linda, who came up from her home in North Carolina, informed me. "We don't have a boat, and we were wondering if you could come over and get us." I obliged her willingly.

Anita outlived Paul by a few more years. She was extremely lonely and growing very weak from heart problems. She, too, went to a nursing home, but she was there only a few weeks before she died.

Again, I received a phone call from Linda and Janet. "Would you please once more do us a favor? Mother, too, wanted to be cremated and have her ashes scattered in the Hudson." Again, I obliged. We rowed out to the middle and Linda did the honors. A brief prayer was said. And then Janet made a most interesting observation regarding the way their folks had bickered over the years.

"You know," she said, "the way mother and father got along, I wouldn't be at all surprised if the tide was going south when Father's ashes were put into the river and that when Mother's went in, the tide was going north!" To me that was a most amusing observation.

Eleanora

My older brother Larry spent most of his working life as a merchant mariner. Over the years, he befriended a host of people, some of whom were downright characters.

Eleanora was a bar fly who was the current "friend" of one of Larry's associates, and she accompanied her boyfriend for a weekend visit to the homestead. In those days (the late '70s and into the '80s), Sandy would put the younger children into bed in the evening and then we would share the evening with Larry and Torill and their guests, sitting in front of a roaring fireplace and enjoying cocktails. Our sessions often went on until daybreak. It was a most memorable and enjoyable period in our married lives.

Eleanora was an obnoxious character. She would make the most insulting comments without knowing any better. Initially, we thought she might be an experienced critic, but later we chalked up her conversation to sheer ignorance.

When being taken through the house, she asked Sandy what we did to preserve the flooring. "We use deck paint on it about every three years or so." Sandy told her.

"Deck paint!" Eleanor exclaimed, "What the hell is wrong with you? On these floors you should be using varnish!" That's when we first got an inkling that we were hosting a very abrasive guest.

Next was her comment about the piano. When she spied it in the poolroom she asked me to play something for her. I dutifully complied with her request. When I finished, Eleanora remarked, "Your playing isn't bad, but that piano is grossly out of tune. Why don't you do yourself a favor? Get an axe and chop it up!" I thought of explaining that tuning the piano was virtually useless because the homestead had no central heating and that the dampness and extreme changes in temperature wrecked havoc on the instrument, but what the hell. The lady was boorish, and it wasn't worth reasoning with her.

It was my misfortune to stumble over the pronouncement of her name, and she would patiently correct me, at first. I kept calling her "Eleanor" and not "El-e-a-nor-a," which she preferred. After several of these errors, she blurted out to me, "Look, honey, you seem to be having a lot of difficulty with my name. Why don't you just call me by my handle, Sunny?" Those were the days when CB sets were in vogue and all of the users had pet names referred to as a "handle." "Sunny" it was for the rest of Eleanora's stay.

We had one consolation: she was only with us two days!

The Midnight Phone Calls

It was another of those many evenings when Larry and Torill and Sandy and I were sitting in front of a comforting fire as we sipped our cocktails. The midnight hour had passed when the ringing telephone interrupted our conversation.

I answered it.

"John," a frantic voice slurred, "this is Martha. I'm at the club, and I need a ride home. Would you please come and get me?"

I politely explained to the caller that she had the wrong number. I returned to the living room and told the others about the phone call. We engaged in further conversation for a few minutes when the phone rang once again.

Once again, I answered it.

"John, this is Martha. Please come and get me. I'm at the club and I'm in no condition to drive," she said in an even more obviously slurred voice.

"Martha, you have the wrong number. Please don't dial here again," I directed.

Back I came into the living room, and we resumed our conversation after I related the content of the second phone call.

Again the phone rang.

I picked up the receiver to once more hear her familiar voice. "John, what is keeping you? I've been waiting here at the club, and I want to come home." It was hard to believe that she had dialed the wrong number three times in a row.

"Martha," I said with some degree of exasperation, "You have once again dialed the same wrong number. Please take the time to look up the right one in the phone directory. Don't call this number again!

Back to the fireside. By this time we were all getting a kick out of the repeated wrong number calls.

When the phone rang the fourth time, Larry suggested, "Let me handle it this time." Since the phone was located in the adjacent kitchen, he stretched the extension cord to reach the living room so that we could all hear what he had to say.

Of course it was Martha. Larry interrupted her plea and said reassuringly, "Martha, this is John. I'll be there to pick you up in less than fifteen minutes."

We never heard from Martha again. For all we know she may still be waiting at the club!

The Porno Call

I have always been gullible. I am also guilty of being a little slow on the uptake, not recognizing signals until too late and not particularly adept at thinking on my feet. Days after a contentious argument, a clever rejoinder I should have made will come to mind. These traits occasionally caused me problems, such as the time when, home alone, I received an unusual phone call.

"Mr. Stevens," the voice on the other end of the line said, "Would you please take a minute or two to assist me in answering a few survey questions?"

Ordinarily I would terminate this type of call at the outset. For some reason, the voice at the other end of the line had a tone of sincerity. I decided to go along, since at the time I had a few minutes to spare.

"Go ahead, fire away!" I responded.

"How old are you, sir?" he asked

"Sir. I like that, "I thought to myself. " It shows respect."

"Forty-five," I answered.

"Do you enjoy movies?"

"As a matter of fact, we do."

"This is turning out to be a piece of cake," I thought to myself.

"Have you ever attended an R-rated movie?" the surveyor continued.

"Oops! An odd question. A bit too familiar," said I to myself.

"One," I truthfully responded.

"Did you like it?"

"Somewhat," I guardedly said.

"Do you like having sex with your wife?"

"Very much so," I confessed.

"How frequently do you have sex?" "Approximately once a week," I replied.

"Sir, I'm an experienced porno star. Does that make a difference to you?"

"Not really, but could you wind this down? I haven't much time left to spend on the phone," I said.

"Do you know anything about oral sex?" he inquired.

"You're treading on thin ice, here," I responded. I'm not going to answer that question, and I don't appreciate the drift of this conversation."

"I'm sorry, sir," he apologized and then asked, "Do you love your wife very much?"

"Yes, I do."

"Do you know about anal sex?"

"Can we cut this short? Yes, I've heard about anal sex."

"What would you say if I told you I have a twelve-inch penis?" he inquired.

"That's it! No more of this stuff, buster!" I huffed.

"Please sir, I'm just taking a survey," he pleaded.

"Then finish it up, but without the personal questions, please." I retorted.

"Do you think your wife would enjoy having sex with me?" he asked.

"Time for me to hang up on him," I decided. But by this time I was wondering just how far he would go, so I continued listening.

"I don't think she would," I said.

"Why not?" he asked.

"We both consider sex to be a very private thing between us," I stated firmly.

"Would you mind watching me have sex with your wife," he continued.

"That's it! End of conversation! Don't call back or I'll contact the police," I warned him.

I hung up, disgusted but somewhat amused by the whole gist of my very first porno phone conversation ever.

Not being able to contain myself, I phoned Sandy at work.

"Honey, I just finished responding to an interesting phone survey that took a couple of weird turns. It might lead to problems affecting you," I informed her.

"In what way," she asked.

"Well, I'm not exactly sure, but I think I may have made an appointment for you to have anal sex with an ex-porno star with a twelve-inch dick—while I watch," I explained.

Her response was immediate, "Not tonight dear; I have a headache!"

The Couch Potato

Brad Paine was one of my daughter's friends. What she saw in him, I'll never know. He was an aimless sort, and he talked endlessly about nothing. For several months, he seemed to adopt us as family, and he treated us accordingly. He would come to our house after school, turn on the TV, stretch himself on the couch, and proceed to watch some obnoxious show. Sometimes he'd even raid the refrigerator.

This routine truly irritated me, but at first I wasn't willing to make an issue of it. I would even engage in idle conversation with Brad if I happened to return from the college in the late afternoon while he was still hanging out at our house. Although not much of a TV fan, I would sometimes just sit and stare at the boob tube, hoping the boy would leave.

One afternoon, Brad was absent-mindedly watching a sitcom when the usual string of ads appeared on the screen. One depicted some new kind of miracle concoction that would remove warts.

Brad suddenly sat up and took notice. "Mr. Stevens, can I please use your telephone," he asked. There's an important call I need to make right now."

He dialed a number and began talking in a hurried manner, "Aunt Pat, is that you? Good. Listen, Aunt Pat, right now I'm watching an important ad on TV that you really need to see. Turn on your TV to Channel 10 right now! It's all about how to get rid of warts like all of those ugly ones on your face!" I couldn't believe what I was hearing the boy say.

Aunt Pat must have had the same reaction as I did. She spoke loudly and clearly into the phone. Loud enough for me to hear what she had to say.

"Brad, where are you?" she asked.

"I'm up at the Stevens house," he answered.

"And so now all of Rensselaer will know about the warts on my face. Damn you, Brad, why don't you just use your head sometimes?" She hung up on him.

At least it got him to leave the house.

<u>Uncle Lou and Aunt Nora — Tigers on the Highway</u>

Sandy had an Uncle Lou, her dad's brother, who had disappeared off the family radar screen decades ago, and no one knew where he was. In his late 80s, he contacted his family and filled in the missing information. Somehow, he and Sandy's folks had drifted apart over some minor issue, and Lou had moved out of state. He had married, become a widower, and remarried.

Lou's current wife, Nora, had instigated the resuming of relationships. She tried to contact Sandy's dad, but he had passed away, and Millie, Sandy's mom, was in failing health. Nora and Lou were living comfortably in a retirement community near Orlando, Florida, and they invited Sandy and her brother to visit them anytime they were in the area.

The visits were unforgettable experiences.

Lou and Nora were enjoying their golden years and had established a life style to their liking. It included dining out, always at the same Bob Evans chain restaurant. They went there because they had a favorite waitress and because the food was tasty and inexpensive.

Getting to and from the restaurant was the interesting part.

Uncle Lou insisted upon driving, and it was a terrifying experience to be a passenger. He was always behind the wheel with Nora next to him in the passenger seat.

At home, it was apparent that Lou was battling the frailties of a ninety-year-old. He could barely get around the house, because his legs were giving out. He would manage by limping around the house using his cane, and clutching chairs and tables to keep himself upright. His mind was good, but his body wasn't. Yet, when it came to driving, he insisted on getting behind the wheel, and he would not be deterred.

"I have a hell of a time walking," he confessed, "but get me behind the wheel and I'm as good as gold."

That was his side of the story.

Sister-in-law Laura had some horror stories to tell. She and Sandy's brother, Bill, had managed to survive a few excursions to Bob Evans with Lou and Nora.

"Nora was the co-pilot," Laura related. "In addition, she was also the navigator, and she gave way to no one. The old people insisted upon driving at a modest speed in the passing lane, much to the chagrin of other drivers. Nora was relentless when it came to staying ahead of the other vehicles.

"Watch it, Lou!" she'd warn. "There's one trying to pass you on the right. CUT HIM OFF, LOU!"

Fortunately, the other driver was driving defensively and decided to drop back before being driven into the ditch.

On a later occasion, Laura and Bill were once again riding in the back seat, quivering with fear since their earlier experiences with Lou at the wheel.

"Lou, you missed the turn-off for Bob Evans. Turn around and head back the other way!" Laura commanded. When they came to the next intersection Lou screeched into a Uey. The problem, however, was the looming aspect of a huge semi barreling down on Uncle Lou's car as it swerved into the lane ahead of the giant truck.

Suddenly there was the loud screeching of air brakes accompanied by the cacophony of the truck's air horn. Laura could see the truck driver's eyes bulging with terror as his hands gripped the steering wheel. She and Bill were convinced that the end had come.

Miraculously what would surely have been a fatal accident did not occur. Somehow the truck driver managed to swerve into the far lane and avoid the crash.

The reaction from Nora: "Boy, Lou, you sure scared the hell out of him!"

Laura was traumatized just describing the near-death experience.

At a later occasion, Sandy and I had lunch with Lou and Nora. When I saw him inching around the house, I was reminded of Laura's forewarnings. Nevertheless, Sandy and I acceded to Lou's insistence upon driving and came out of the experience unscathed.

Not long after our visit, Lou and Nora moved to Illinois to stay with Nora's daughter. A year or two after that we received word that the couple had passed away—never to be forgotten, however.

Lidfen and the Young Maiden

My older brother Larry traveled extensively during his career as an engineering officer in the Merchant Marines. Since he was friendly and outgoing, he shared many of his friendships by bringing home several people over the years.

One most memorable visitor was Lidfen, a young man from Norway. This tall, handsome, well-educated young guy in his mid-twenties had an extraordinary sense of humor. He just happened to be at loose ends at that time in his life.

When not at sea, brother Larry engaged in a number of engineering projects on the riverbank of our property. He had received permission from the Army Corps of Engineers to build two sturdy erosion barriers, since the Hudson River had been wearing away our property for decades.

He needed physical help, more than other family members were able to give because of job commitments, etc.

Larry suggested to Lidfen that he might be interested in coming to the USA for several months. He would have free room and board at our homestead and would be paid a minimal wage. Lidfen, young and free, eagerly accepted the offer.

Thus began a fondly remembered chapter in the lives of several of us who came to know our new Norwegian friend. Lidfen had completed college and had a fine command of the English language. He was spending his time at a not-very- demanding job in a shipping agent's office, and he wanted a change.

It didn't take long to develop a friendship with this likeable guy, who was very socially adept. We were pleased to invite him along on an endless number of outings. He loved to ski and to drink beer and to flirt with single women.

The Larsens, who lived across the river, asked Larry and Sandy and me to a house party. They had met Lidfen and had thoroughly enjoyed his company, and they asked if we would bring him along. They had also invited along an unmarried niece, a young schoolteacher who just might be interesting company for Lidfen.

The Larsen party was one of those perfect occasions where the ambiance and conversation were stimulating and upbeat. After Lidfen was introduced to the young lady, it became obvious that he had sparked her interest. I'm not sure the fascination was reciprocated, but Lidfen was polite and attentive.

After libations and some great refreshments, everyone present relaxed and engaged in conversation. At one point, after she had surmised that their relationship was evolving, the young lady directed this unusual question to the Norwegian guest.

"How do you say sex in Norwegian?" she coyly inquired.

To which he immediately responded, "It depends on what type of sex you are interested in."

Her jaw literally dropped, and she withdrew from conversation for the rest of the evening.

Over the months, he stayed with us, and on subsequent visits, Lidfen's quick wit delighted us.

An Amazing Mother-in-law was Millie

So many adjustments have to be worked out when you marry. New lifestyle, new demands, new attitudes, new people. For Sandy and me, the adjustments were minor, mostly interesting and fun, and in no small way attributable to Sandy's mother, Millie.

What a unique lady! She was an excellent cook and housekeeper. She loved working as cosmetologist, applying to herself the added affectations of green eye shadow and auburn colored hair. She kept trim. And she loved the social life: horseracing, dancing, cocktails, and parties. A really fun person. In later life, she even weathered a leg amputation — caused by poor circulation due to excessive smoking.

In money matters, Millie was totally impractical. If she wanted something, she bought it. Gifts for the children and grandchildren were never spared. She wasn't averse to treating herself well either. She had a mink stole and glittering costume jewelry. She would occasionally put on airs by using Bostonian verbal affectations in public, like "hoff" for half.

One time she wanted money for wall-to-wall carpeting. Sandy's dad dug in his heels and refused the request as unaffordable at the time. Then he made the mistake of leaving town on a business trip. When he arrived home, a sea of spanking new pink carpeting throughout greeted him as he stepped through the door.

"Come to think of it," I mused, "the genetic connection between Sandy and her mother in this situation was almost scary. Years later in our married life, Sandy had demanded a brand new car for herself. She was weary of driving well-used and abused cars that often broke down. I had successfully delayed the action, using affordability as an excuse. But Sandy had her own job at a nursing home. As you may have guessed, I made the mistake of taking the children away to my sister-in-law's camp for a summer vacation in the Adirondacks. When I returned, a shiny new Plymouth was parked in the driveway.

"How can we afford this new car?" I whined.

"That's my problem," Sandy retorted. "I bought this car in my own name, and I intend to pay for it myself!"

The Knitting Needles

As her health declined in the later years, Millie kept up her handcraft talents and she also retained her sense of humor. She had always been a whiz at crochet work as well as at knitting, never refusing a request to make a gift for a wedding or for a baby shower.

It was in the middle of a dull winter when the "knitting needle" incident occurred. Millie and I were the only ones at home. As I descended the stairs from the second floor, I looked into the living room to observe Millie industriously knitting away, something she seemingly had been doing as long as I could remember.

"The lady is amazing," I thought. "There she is, hard at work at a labor of love in spite of her dimming eye sight and arthritic fingers. What a wonderful, thoughtful person.

Little did I realize that Millie was hating the job at hand. Her daughter-in-law, Laura, had asked her to make an afghan that involved working mostly with navy blue and other dark colors that were particularly difficult for the old lady to distinguish. She wouldn't refuse to do the job, but she wasn't enjoying it at all.

"Mother, you seem to be doing a great job on that afghan. How is it coming along?" I asked.

That question unleashed a flood of pent -up stress. "You want to know how it's coming along?" she responded. "I'll tell you just how it's coming along. I hate the goddamned thing. I'd like to take this whole business, needles and all, and shove it right up Laura's ass!"

I never again brought up the progress on the afghan.

Keeping us on the run:

In her widowed years, Millie was in poor financial straits, so much so that when her husband died she had no choice but to stay with her children. Her son and his wife took care of her for the most part, and that wasn't easy for Millie nor for Laura and Bill. Once in a while, Sandy and I would share the responsibility. It wasn't easy for us, either, because there were five children living at home and there was only the one bathroom at the family's disposal. Nevertheless, it would not have been fair for Sandy's brother to have the frail, elderly lady all the time. Sometimes she could be downright challenging.

Millie's stays with the Stevens family were always an experience. For one thing, she was the type of person who seemed to thrive on keeping people on the run.

For example: "If you're going to the store, dear," (she called everyone "dear") she would say, "would you please remember to get me some cigarettes! Don't make a special trip, dear."

Out I would go, making a quick dash to the nearby minimart.

"Here are your cigarettes, Mill. No trouble at all," I would say.

"Thank you very much, dear," she would respond. "Did you remember to get me some gum drops?"

She hadn't asked for gumdrops. How could I be expected to pick up something she hadn't asked for? Thence there would be another quick trip to the minimart.

"Here are your gumdrops, Mother," I would say when I returned.

"That's nice dear," she would say. "Did you remember to pick up doughnuts for breakfast?"

Chagrinned, I would reply, "I'll run out to get the doughnuts later on."

While I was making the runs to the minimart, daughter Vicky would have been dispatched upstairs to get Millie's yarn, son Greg would have been requested to empty and clean out her ashtray, daughter Giss would have been asked to make an appointment with Millie's hairdresser, and daughter Jenn would be off getting the old lady some ribbon.

I didn't forget the doughnuts. When I returned with the breakfast goodies, she asked, "Would it be too much trouble to run out and get me a box of Kleenex, dear?"

Jenn returned with the ribbon and was promptly dispatched to go out and bring back ice cream. Giss, having successfully made the hair appointment, was sent upstairs to get Millie a towel. Vicky was asked to take

Mother's used coffee cup to the kitchen, and Greg, fresh from cleaning the ashtray, was asked to get pills from Millie's overnight bag.

The following day, when I returned home from teaching my classes, Mother was waiting. "If you go out, dear, would you please remember to get me some Polident?"

Talk about perpetuity!!

The Pillow Incident

On some occasions, Millie would stay a few days at a time with us. If she spent too much time with our large family, the children would drive her insane— and vice versa. When her mother stayed over, Sandy would pack two children into one bed so that Millie could have a bedroom of her own.

Daughter Heather had developed the annoying habit of sneaking into her parents' bedroom and stealing the most comfortable pillow for herself, swapping it for a mushy one. This stealth mission would take place in the late afternoon while her parents were working or otherwise occupied. The recipient of the mushy pillow would exchange it right back as soon as the ruse was discovered. Heather's devious stunt was no secret.

The pillow-exchanging routine had been going on for months before Millie arrived to stay a few days. At this stage, Millie was quite frail, extremely thin, and dependent upon a wooden leg she'd received after the amputation.

Heather had been assigned to sleep with Jenn. It wasn't always Heather who lost her bed. Sandy tried to be fair about inconveniencing the same child too often.

For me, this routine of shifting people into different bedrooms was quite confusing. I could never remember which child was to sleep with whom or which bedroom would be occupied by Millie. It was inevitable that this would eventually result in a mix up.

One night, when Sandy was doing the all-night shift at the adult nursing home, I had the opportunity to have a few beers with my brother at the local pub, a rare and much enjoyed change of pace. It was well after midnight when I woozily returned home, found my way up the stairs, and entered my bedroom. All was fine until I plumped the pillow, which was downright mushy.

"Damned Heather," I muttered to myself. "She's taken my pillow again. Well, I'll fix her wagon, middle of the night or not!

I strode across the hall to where Heather usually slept. Of course, Heather wasn't in her room. Millie was the occupant, but I had no way of knowing that.

"Give me that goddamned pillow," I barked, grabbing the pillow by its corner and yanking it forcefully from under Millie's head. The poor old dear was bewildered and frightened by the sudden intrusion in the middle of the night.

"I'm sorry, dear, I'd didn't take your pillow," the poor thing whimpered.

I really must have frightened her, because she sat up in bed, attached the wooden leg, and hobbled to the bathroom to relieve herself.

Nighttime Shenanigans

It wasn't too many weeks following the pillow incident that a similar occurrence, much tawdrier in nature, occurred.

The setting was similar to the pillow incident: Millie as guest in a bedroom, Sandy working the overnight shift, me having a few beers with my brother. This time around, Sandy had arranged for Millie to sleep in our bed.

I had been designated to sleep on the downstairs couch, but those directions were soon forgotten after the seventh or eighth beer.

It was in the wee hours when I tiptoed into the house and up to my own bedroom. Removing every stitch of my clothing, I slyly slid under the bed clothing and pressed my body against someone I thought to be my wife.

As my amorous inclinations increased, I coyly ran my hands over the stomach of my sleeping partner, Millie. I thought that my bed partner seemed a little wrinkled and close to the bone.

"It's me, dear," Millie said. "I don't think you're supposed to be sleeping with me tonight."

Horrified by my own behavior, I bolted downstairs to the couch.

Florence the Ingrate

Florence Layden was a unique lady — truly unique. She was feisty, outspoken, aggressive and as much of an ingrate as one could ever know. However, she was also a lot of fun because of, or maybe in spite of, her abrasiveness. She smoked and she swore and she seldom had a nice word for anyone. And, oh boy, did she enjoy a good stiff Manhattan on the rocks! She could get away with all of this because she was over 90.

We'd met at church through a mutual friend some ten years earlier. I used to admire her regal bearing and her stately features. She did a good job with makeup, too, particularly rouge. Her hair was snow white, and she depended upon her cane to help her get around—and also to use as a prop. A maiden lady, she had worked as a sales clerk at various Albany department stores earlier on. She lived in a low-income housing project and was just about making it on her paltry social security and some welfare.

Her method of operation was to impose upon people, relying on their good graces, and if she didn't get those, she'd browbeat people into submission with insults, guilt trips — the works. When some poor soul broke down and asked her to lunch or dinner, she would often badmouth them to others, which, of course, meant she would badmouth me to others, as well. For instance, she once said, "Virginia had me over for dinner. It took her long enough to get around to inviting me. And do you know what we had to eat? Hamburgers! I hate hamburgers!" Or another time, "Evelyn picked me up and took me for a Sunday drive. And don't you know, she had to bring along her brats. They were so noisy in the car, I couldn't stand it."

Ah, the essence of Florence.

The Lenten Service

It has long been a tradition in our church to have a solemn and pensive evening Lenten service. At the end of the service, all of the lighting is dimmed and all of the church attendants leave silently at the end of the service. It's been done that way for decades.

And so it was at this particular Lenten service. All was going as usual, until they dimmed the lights.

"Who in *hell* turned down those lights?" came a very audible voice from the south aisle. It was Florence, and she loudly continued, "I'm an old lady and I can't see nothing."

Boy, was she a peach!

The Front Porch Dilemma

The fact of the matter is that Florence wore thin, even in a short time.

Our most memorable get-together was on a Sunday afternoon in late August not many months before Florence passed away. She'd asked herself to dinner, as she often did. Sandy and I had been able to defer it as long as possible, but eventually Florence wore us down. We knew she wasn't at all fond of children, and we had seven of them to irritate her. It just so happened that during the early afternoon, Sandy had been preserving tomatoes in mason jars, and so she was too busy help me entertain Florence.

No sooner was she seated on the front porch than Florence announced, "I want a Manhattan."

"Coming up," I complied, starting toward the kitchen. I was wary of Florence because her physical condition had deteriorated markedly over the recent past. She could possibly fall as a result of a dizzy spell. She assured me that she would stay in the rocking chair until I returned.

Upon my return, our conversation resumed. Florence always had something to say, usually in the form of complaints sprinkled with curse words. Complaints about the apartment complex manager where she lived: "He's a lazy bastard!" Complaints about her illnesses. Complaints about her rotten friends who never had her over for dinner. On and on it went. Somehow the Manhattan, followed by another, made it all bearable for me. I have to admit that she was one feisty lady—and never, never dull.

"I'm ready for another one," she announced, thrusting her glass toward me.

"Do you think you should? You're not getting any younger, you know. I'm afraid you might have a fall and break your hip," I warned.

"Be sure to put enough ice in it," was Florence's response.

While savoring her third cocktail, she abruptly announced, "Bill, I've got to pee!"

I thought to myself, "Oh boy, what do I do now. She'll never make it up the stairs to the only bathroom in the house." I shared this concern with my guest.

Florence pondered for a moment. "I have an idea. Why don't you bring out one of those mason jars that Sandy is using to do up tomatoes? I'll pee into that." She followed that suggestion up with, "You'd better hurry. I can't hold it much longer."

I collected my thoughts. The old girl wanted to let go right on the front porch in broad daylight for all the neighbors to see. Then I had a bright idea. To resolve the problem, I took a blanket out of the closet.

"Florence, I want you to wrap this blanket around your shoulders to cover yourself. Be sure to let it drape down all around you so that you will have privacy. In the meantime, I'll get a mason jar from the kitchen." I was amazed at my own acumen.

When I returned to the porch with the jar, the old lady had already dropped her drawers to the floor and was clutching the blanket around her.

At that time a logistical problem reared its ugly head. Florence couldn't hold the blanket around her and hold the mason jar at the same time.

"I'll hold the blanket. You hold the jar," she declared.

I was gripped with angst. "This means I have to hold the jar up to the source of the water, I suddenly realized. "Ugh!"

Down on one knee I went, turning my head away from her withered crotch while holding the jar far up between her legs. I must admit, however, to taking a sneak peak at the wispy silver hairs. Then I felt a warm stream of water begin to flow into the jar—except for a small trickle that missed the jar and ran down over my fingers and down my arm, dripping off my elbow. "This has to be the most miserable experience of my life," I mused.

"Why is this happening to me?" I wondered. "How could I ever have let myself get into this predicament?" I wanted to throw up — or cry — or both.

The final straw was when Florence gently stroked my head while I was holding the jar. "You're just like a son to me," she cooed.

Eventually the ordeal ended.

"That will never, ever happen to me again in my life," I vowed to myself.

The Hairnet Fiasco

Inevitably, Florence's health failed to the point where she had to be put in a nursing home. This didn't stop her from demanding endless favors from her friends, who would meekly comply because (a) they felt sorry for her and (b) they didn't want to be badmouthed all around Albany.

One blustery winter night with near-blizzard conditions, I received a frantic phone call from Florence.

"Bill, you've got to help me! I can't find my hairnet and I won't go to bed without it. I want you to bring me another one. *Now!*"

"Florence, have you heard the weather report?" I said, trying to reason with her. "It's terrible out there. The snow is coming down like crazy, and the driving conditions are awful."

"I don't care! I need a hairnet and I need it now!" she demanded.

"I must be crazy," I said to myself as I drove toward the nursing home with the hairnet in a little bag at my side.

When I arrived, I found I was the third person to visit Florence that evening. Each of the others had also brought along a hairnet just to shut the old lady up.

"If she doesn't die soon, I just might kill her," I told myself.

The Funeral Parlor Episode

Eventually Florence died. I had power of attorney and had promised to take care of the funeral arrangements. Florence had paid for and arranged her own funeral years in advance, which saved me a lot of problems. She was laid out in a lovely pink gown, with just the right amount of rouge on her cheeks. She looked so much at peace.

I agreed to drive Marie Blake, one of Florence's oldest friends and a professional hairdresser, to the wake.

What happened when we walked up to the casket was bizarre.

Marie put her hand up to her mouth and said aloud, "Oh, dear Florence, what have they done to your hair? You never liked it that way. Here, let me fix it."

With that Marie began undoing Florence's curls and rearranging them in a style Marie thought was more suitable. Other wake attendants stared in astonishment as Marie continued with her mission.

"You know," I said to myself, "this is truly macabre, but I think if Florence is looking down on all of this, she's getting quite a kick out of it!"

My Unique Lady Doctor

In the late 1980s, I began to have occasional pains in my lower jaw that lasted only a minute or so but were most worrisome. It happened once while I was singing in the choir at a Sunday service and then again several months later while riding in my boat on the Hudson River. It may have occurred more often than that, but those were the most memorable attacks.

I happened to have a great friend of many years who had a job as office manager for a female cardiologist. When I mentioned my jaw pains to my good friend, she heartily suggested that I make an appointment with her employer, Dr. Jana Hoffmeir. This lady was to become my health guru for nearly two decades. She also became a very close friend, probably because of her expertise and her caring manner, as well as her terrific sense of humor.

What immediately attracted me to her was her no-nonsense, deeply concerned manner. She spoke with a pronounced Czech accent, which definitely added to the lighter side of our visits. Over the years, I had a few catherizations and two bypass operations, all of which were very competently managed by this exemplary cardiologist.

I had never before had an appointment with a female physician, so this was a first, and I recall it clearly.

She suspected that my jaw aches were "silent" heart attacks, and she had had me schedule a blood test a few weeks before our first consultation.

Harvard on the Hudson

The Blood Test

During our first meeting, she scanned my test results and commented in that inimitable Czech accent, "You haff too much sugar in your blood."

I immediately went on the defensive by saying, "It's after Halloween, and I probably had too much Halloween candy!"

"Vhy are you lying? You had your blood tested many weeks in advance of Halloveen!"

I was trapped and had no recourse. Then and there I decided that this wise old bird knew her stuff and wouldn't be taking any nonsense. I knew that she was someone I could rely upon for my health care from then on.

When talking with my older brother who was also having some health concerns, I suggested he make an appointment with my new doctor, Jana Hoffmeir. He took my advice, and like me, he was promptly scheduled for a blood test before his first consultation.

I had not told him about my initial conversation involving the Halloween candy and also the attempted cover-up, which she so cleverly thwarted, so he had no idea about my blood sugar lie.

When he appeared for his appointment, Dr. Hoffmeir detected a problem with my brother's blood test.

"You haff too much sugar in your blood," she announced.

"It's just after Easter and I ate a lot of Easter candy," he said, reaching for an excuse.

For a moment she just stared at him, probably recalling my attempt to cover up using the Halloween candy excuse.

"Do you know vhat I am tinking vhile you are talking?" she asked with that Eastern European tone. "I am tinking — bullshit!" That won him over, too.

For several years, my brother and I would compare our experiences at the doctor's office. Visits with her became something to look forward to. It became obvious, likewise, that she thoroughly enjoyed our appointments.

The Christmas Card

It had long become a custom for me to send out a lengthy Christmas letter that sometimes ran as much a dozen pages. The content was a review of the previous year's events involving family, local, and national news, etc. I would more or less keep a diary throughout the year by writing down interesting occurrences in my life. In addition to the newsletter, the package would include a photograph I had taken of something worth remembering.

I added Dr. Hoffmeir to my Christmas card list. One year, the photograph was of my two older brothers and me enjoying a boat ride on the Hudson River during the summer season. Each of us had a cigar in our mouth, and each was holding up a cup of beer. It was a cameo of three guys having a thoroughly good time.

Several days after Christmas, my phone rang.

"This is Dr. Hoffmeir," came that familiar Czech accent. "Vhat are you doing smoking cigars and drinking beer? Don't you know that is bad for your heart?"

It was easy to detect that the admonishment was being delivered by someone who was thoroughly enjoying herself.

The Ladder Incident

One time my brother and I were working on the garage roof. The job required a ladder, and brother Barry had climbed up a few rungs in order to do some carpentry work.

I decided to move my pickup truck. Unfortunately I failed to see that the rear bumper of the truck was very close to the ladder. When I pulled forward, the bumper caught the ladder and pulled it away from the garage. Brother Barry fell a few feet and landed on the ground. He wasn't seriously injured.

Later that week, he had a routine checkup with Dr. Hoffmeir. During their conversation, he happened to mention the ladder incident.

A few weeks later, I, too, was scheduled for a routine checkup. Her first comment as I entered her office was, "Vhat is this I hear about you causing your brother to fall off a ladder. I vant you to know that it is *my* job to kill my own patients." How great it was to have a doctor with a fine sense of humor.

The Prostate Checkup

Once, after I had been her patient for a few years, Dr. Hoffmeir asked, "Haff you ever had your prostate checked?"

"As a matter of fact, I haven't," I confessed, recalling clearly that two of my older brothers, Kim and Bleek, had prostate problems and that brother Bleek had died from prostate cancer in the recent past.

"Vell, I started out as a general practitioner before I became a cardiologist. I am going to give you a basic prostate test right now!"

I wasn't looking forward to the experience. My understanding was that having a finger in one's rectum wasn't something to look forward to.

She proceeded with the examination.

While in the process I commented to her, "You know, I'm really not enjoying this."

Her response: "I suppose you think I am?!"

The Colonoscopy

Prostate checkups are quite routine and not all that uncomfortable. Not so a colonoscopy.

Harvard on the Hudson

Brother Larry had had two serious bouts with colon cancer. Dr. Hoffmeir wasn't taking any chances with me. She wrote a prescription for pre-procedure medication, which turned out to be a whole gallon of the damnedest tasting stuff. I had a choice between a cherry and a lemon flavor. I picked the cherry, but I don't think the lemon would have been any better.

The instructions read that the day before my outpatient appointment for the colonoscopy at the hospital, I should consume the entire gallon by taking one eight-ounce glass at a time until it was completely consumed. The instructions also cautioned that I should stay close to the toilet that entire day,

I consumed two or three glasses, leaving about a half hour between each glassful. At first it wasn't too bad, but the fun part soon wore off. By the fourth glass, I was gagging. Two hours had passed and I was witnessing no physical effects. So I decided to run a few errands. It was summertime, and I looked forward to taking a spin in my 1931 Model A Ford Roadster with the top down.

The first stop would be at my church in Albany. I'd been serving for years as treasurer and made it a point to stop by to pick up the mail two or three times a week. All was going just fine until I passed the Palace Theater in Albany and cranked the steering wheel hard to the left in order to make the turn toward church. That simple act caused an intestinal cramp that was devastating! I felt my bowels release—like opening up the flood gates—and my intestines exuded what felt like warm oatmeal. Lots of it! At the time, I was wearing sweat pants that had elastic at the ankles, thank heaven.

There would be no stopping at the church; that was for sure. The only recourse was to head for home as quickly as possible. On the way back across the river, I took another minor turn and a second volley let go. By this time I felt as though I had warm oatmeal up to my knees. And it happened a third and a fourth time before I reached my driveway at home.

When I opened the door, I suddenly recalled that I had invited a visiting friend from Florida to stop by and do her laundry. Sure enough, she was right there in the toilet/laundry room just inside the doorway.

"Renee, you have got to get out of here now!" I exclaimed. "I have a very serious problem, and it needs to be taken care of immediately!" Obligingly, she hastened into the living room, while I took care of the ugliest mess I've ever encountered. So much for not heeding the warning on the prescription.

The colonoscopy procedure itself was a breeze. Within an hour or so, it was over, and I had suffered little discomfort.

Some years later, I was scheduled for another one. This time, however, the preparation was much simpler. All I had to do was consume a small bottle of liquid the day before the procedure. The instructions indicated that I was to stay close to the john, and I can assure you that I followed them to the letter!

The Pillow Gag

In my later years, I have become very fond of wearing running (sweat) suits. They are just plain comfortable and so much easier to get in and out of than the more formal attire I was used to wearing to the college and to church.

Dr. Hoffmeir was forever concerned about my weight. "You veigh too much," she would say during just about every office visit. "You should lose at least twenty pounds."

An idea stuck me. For our next appointment, I would stuff a small pillow in the stomach area under my sweat suit. I thought she would get a kick out of it.

At the next appointment, with the pillow well hidden under my sweat suit, I deliberately stood sideways in the doorway as I entered her examining room. At the time she had her head down, studying my medical history.

When she looked up and saw the profile of my extended belly, she just about went into shock.

"Vhat are you doing to yourself!" she exclaimed.

When I removed the pillow, I thought she might collapse, she laughed so hard. As I said previously, visiting this lady was a fun experience.

The Chippendale

Not only was Dr. Hoffmeir a hoot, but her office staff were a fun bunch. Prior to routine examinations, I got to know Marion and Velvet fairly well. Once realizing "the girls" had a sense of humor, I told them that, in my younger days, I had a part-time job as a "Chippendale," one of a team of male strippers. Trying to picture this brought snickers and grins to the office staff, who were dealing with an overweight, bald, and wrinkled septuagenarian. Throughout office visits over the years, we often kidded about my alleged shady past.

After several visits, it occurred to me to surprise the ladies, the doctor included, by showing up at the office in Chippendale outfit. At a local party store, it was easy to find an eye mask. At one time, I'd worn bow ties, so there was a black one among my collection. It wasn't difficult to buy a pair of black briefs at the local K-mart. For extra effect, I tucked a dollar bill or two into the waistband of my shorts and the outfit was complete.

All that was needed was an accomplice to help me pull off the stunt. That's where brother Barry came in. He and I scheduled our visits with the doctor back-to-back one weekday morning. I was attired in the usual running suit with the Chippendale outfit underneath. My brother joined me in the interior waiting room and in the privacy of that room, he helped me take off my outer layers of clothing so that I remained dressed only my "male stripper" getup. I then strode into the outer office.

Harvard on the Hudson

When the receptionists saw me as a Chippendale, they could not contain their mirth. The doctor, hearing the commotion from her own office, stepped out into the outer office to see what was causing the raucous reaction. I was concerned that she might not see the humor in my antics, but she laughed just as much as the others in the office. It was a fun experience, and it couldn't have come off any better than it did. Cameras appeared out of nowhere, and I became a Facebook sensation.

One of the receptionists dialed her husband at work. "John, you have got to get out of your office and come down here right away to see what's going on!" she pleaded.

There was another doctor's office on the other side of the building, and that receptionist couldn't resist coming across the hall. What made it even more fun is that the cleaning lady, a 70+, white-haired, poker-faced soul, saw nothing at all funny about the prank. She thought it was indecent.

CHAPTER TWELVE—POST-RETIREMENT TRAVEL

Once the children had matured and were out of the house, Sandy and I had open travel opportunities. My retirement package included a bundle of back pay for unused sick leave over the years. I was most fortunate never to have been ill enough to lose time at work over the 40 years of my employment, and about $65,000 had accrued that could be put toward my hospitalization costs in future years. There was also a provision that 20% of the cash reserve could be taken out for personal use. That was all we needed to know to plan a number of trips over the years.

Our first sojourn was a return trip to the Melbourne area of Australia, where we took in familiar sights and spent considerable time at the home of friends made in 1965-66.

Harvard on the Hudson

South America

The most memorable travel of all was our trip to South America. Rio de Janeiro, our first stop, was a highlight. Sugarloaf Mountain, El Corcovado (with its mountaintop 30-story statue of Christ), beach scenes, and intriguing food made for a fascinating visit. Our wisest decision was to hire a private taxi for a full day. The cost was $150, but the young driver knew his way around the area, taking us to so many places of interest.

From Rio we flew over to the Brazilian side of Iguazu Falls and spent two overnights at the upscale Cataratas Hotel, overlooking the thundering phenomenon. We availed ourselves of a bus trip to the Paraguay side of the river, where we took a thrilling boat trip near the crest of the falls.

We next flew to Buenos Aires, Argentina. The city wasn't nearly as interesting as Rio, but the broad boulevards, the Evita and Juan Peron palace, and a café where the tango was performed were the highlights. The low point was a reputed boat trip on the Parana River which emptied into the bay on which Buenos Aires was located. The murky brown river meandered through populated areas, but the smell of the water was stultifying. While the tour book we used extolled the interesting features of this not-well-known cruise, it failed to mention that the river was an open sewer. The tour guide suggested that we all breathe through our mouths!!

Before leaving home, I had booked a three-night stay at a ranch in Uruguay. First we rode a hydrofoil across the bay from Buenos Aires to Uruguay and spent an overnight at rustic and attractive Colonia, once a 16th century Portuguese outpost. A bus took us to the ranch, where we had a most relaxing stay. We got to know the proprietress, who enjoyed our company so much that she took us to a larger ranch where we met gauchos and saw a functioning ranch in operation.

I had always been fascinated with the name Montevideo, the capital city of Uruguay — so fascinated that I couldn't wait to hear the word "Montevideo" pronounced by a local. At last the opportunity came as we boarded the rickety miniature bus from the ranch to the metropolis. The bus driver personally took our tickets as we boarded the bus. I heard him mumble "Mmundvdeo" in an almost unrecognizable tone. What a disappointment!! All this anticipation about hearing something pronounced in such a garbled manner!

Montevideo was lovely. From the veranda of our hotel, we could enjoy watching the citizenry parading on the broad promenade, which was set back from the beautiful beach.

The next stopover in the South American tour provided unanticipated excitement. LaPaz is the capital and largest city in Bolivia, the second most (next to Haiti) impoverished country in the Western Hemisphere. We had accommodations there for a few days. Looming majestically over the city was Illimani of the Andes range, some 21,000 feet in altitude.

The air was so thin at LaPaz that it caused headaches for those who weren't used to high altitudes. At restaurants, tourists were encouraged to sip cocaine-laced tea, since the drug took away the headaches. I had no problem at all with the discomfort of headaches, but Sandy suffered considerably. "You don't feel any pain because you recently had a heart by-pass operation," she tartly observed. "You have an increased flow of blood while I don't." She sipped the tea.

Curiosity and the thrill of adventure were to drive a wedge between my wife and me while at LaPaz. In the tour book, I read of a fascinating trip to the remote town of Coroico, several miles from LaPaz. The only way to get there was by taking the perilous North Yungas Road, a 40-mile drive by bus down a steep, mountainside, treacherous dirt road, which descended some 50,000 feet. The tour book warned that this was one of the most dangerous roads anywhere in the world!

If I told Sandy about this in advance, she never would have agreed to go with me. Instead, I described the coffee plantations and lovely orchards surrounding the beautiful hotel that awaited us in Coroico.

We had to take a taxi a few miles through the city to the bus depot, where we would catch the bus to Coroico. Along the way there were vendors standing along the streets selling huge ears of boiled corn and delicious-looking chunks of fried chicken. Some vendors were literally ladling out what looked like grapefruit juice from a pail. People would give them a coin and drink directly out of the ladle and then pass it on to the next customer. To me it looked most inviting, but Sandy was adamant about the unsanitary conditions

We boarded the bus and started the hazardous journey. Sandy and I were seated in the last row on the left side of the bus, which was filled with native Bolivians who smiled through rotting teeth when they saw us board the bus.

Within a mile or two, the road began its steep descent. The dirt surface was rocky, bumpy, and rutted much of the way. It was eerie to see so many commemorative bouquets of flowers dotting the roadside, reminding us of the peril of so many who died when their vehicles cascaded off the road and down the steep mountainside to the valley some 10,000 feet below.

The bus driver proceeded slowly, carefully avoiding rockslides that appeared now and then. At a few locations, I thought the bus had driven into a car wash. The entire vehicle was inundated by waterfalls cascading down from the mountain above. I have to admit, I was scared out of my wits. Sandy sat next to me trembling with tears running down her cheeks. She was even more scared than I was.

Harvard on the Hudson

The road was a single lane all the way. Only occasionally was there a bypass carved into the mountainside. If a vehicle approached from the opposite direction, our bus had to back up if the nearest bypass was behind us. At one hairy location, the bus driver, in broken English, directed Sandy to yell out if she felt the rear wheel of the bus going off the road bank. The Bolivian passengers thought we were a riot sitting in our seats rigid with fear.

After hours of such a horrible riding experience, we finally arrived at Coroico, but not before the bus became mired in rain-filled ruts and we had to slog our way through ankle-deep mud to get to the hotel. While we were relieved to set foot in a safe area, the hotel that awaited us was a disaster. Our room was lighted by a single bulb at the end of a cord hanging from the ceiling. The swimming pool was unheated and hadn't been cleaned in weeks. The chef was a very inexperienced young man who delivered a just-about-raw hamburger to our table. There were no other unreserved hotels in the town, so we were stuck.

That night, Sandy got ahold of the tour book. Stupidly, I had not known enough to tear out the page relating to Coroico. When she read the description of the hazardous road we had traversed she became enraged. "Do you mean to tell me you knew all along that we could have died on that damned bus? How could you do this to me?" I did not have an answer. I didn't dare tell her that I thought it would be thrilling.

"I absolutely refuse to go back up that road!" she declared.

"It's the only way back out of here," I confessed. "There is no air service or any other access road." Things got quiet for a very long time.

Two days later, we hesitantly boarded the bus for the return trip up the mountain. Within a few miles, the bus came to a halt. A massive rockslide had covered the road. All able-bodied passengers got off the bus and started moving the huge rocks that blocked the passage. It took a half hour or so. From there we proceeded to the top of the mountain without further incident.

But we still weren't out of the woods! We took a taxi from the bus stop to get back to our hotel in downtown LaPaz. No sooner had we entered the outskirts of the city than another obstacle appeared. As we proceeded down the street, a gang of young men came running out of a side street. They pelted rocks at our vehicle. One broke the front window, and another crashed against the taxi, close to where Sandy was sitting.

At first we thought we were witnessing first-hand some serious anti-American sentiment. Not so. What we did not know was that there was a taxicab driver strike going on in LaPaz and that our driver was a scab. The mob was trying to penalize him for operating his vehicle during a strike. Fortunately, he out-maneuvered the crowd and delivered us safely to our hotel. This was lucky for us because I have no idea how we would have gotten to our hotel after getting off the bus from Coroico. When we finally arrived there, the taxi driver demanded that I pay for half of the cost of his smashed windshield. I steadfastly refused—until the hotel attendant reminded me that my luggage was locked in the taxi trunk and that the driver could easily drive away unless I came up with the $50 he demanded. I reluctantly anteed up the money.

It was always embarrassing when in future conversations with friends Sandy came forth with, "Did I remember to tell how Bill nearly had me killed in Bolivia?"

From Bolivia we took a bus to Peru. Bolivia is an impoverished country with few of the amenities of modern-day travel. I stopped at an outdoor toilet along the bus route where there were footprints drawn in the dirt with a hole dug between them indicating where to relive my intestines.

Sandy looked out a side window toward the rear of the bus and noticed that the rear wheel had come loose and was jutting out a foot or so from the side of the bus. The axle had broken. Then there was a thud as the body of the bus hit the highway, and after that there was a four-hour wait for another bus.

When our bus approached a wide river where there was no bridge, the passengers disembarked and the bus was driven onto a barge that was pulled across the river by cables. The passengers were loaded onto a separate barge and transported across, where they once more boarded the bus. Apparently, there was a danger that if the bus lurched and toppled into the river, several lives would be lost.

We spent two overnights at Lake Titicaca, the highest elevation navigable lake in the world. The village was populated by many native Bolivians, characterized by their brown derby hats. The natives appeared to be very dour and unfriendly to Caucasians. Taking photos was forbidden. The first hotel I had booked was so primitive that we moved to a better one forthwith.

Eventually we arrived in Peru, where we stayed a few days in the ancient Incan Empire capital city of Cusco. It was a nice enough place, but the poverty was rampant. Sandy was particularly distressed about the plight of the children who were forever hawking wares for money, usually postcards or food.

We went to Peru to see Machu Picchu, the royal Inca city far up on a secluded mountain in the Andes. The site was so well obscured that it was not discovered until 1911. The ancient civilization was most advanced. The intricate stonework and terracing shed light on a city that had thrived several centuries previously. Sandy and I spent two overnights there, giving in to the temptation to buy such souvenirs as huge preserved tarantulas inside plastic boxes.

Peru and Brazil were certainly the highlights of our South American adventure. From Peru, we flew back to Bolivia and then toward Rio. It was on this leg of the flight that a passenger from a tourist group looked out the plane widow and noticed a large gaping hole about a foot in diameter in the wing of our transport. She called the tour director, who notified the flight attendant of the potential crisis. The plane landed at the next available airport. Apparently the hole in the wing had been covered with duct tape, which blew loose during the flight. The airline officials wanted to put more tape over the hole, but the tour director insisted that another plane be substituted, and she got her way, thank heaven.

That trip to South America would last forever in our memories.

Portugal

When a close friend came home from his honeymoon and raved about Portugal, I knew Sandy and I would have to go there some day. Within a few years after retirement, we went for a ten-day stay. My recollections of our few days in Lisbon include a hotel in the center of the city where we were awakened in the wee hours by the clang and clatter of bottles and cans as the trash was being collected down the street. On the positive side was the visit to a 17th century museum containing ornate carriages used by royalty at the time. We strolled around the cramped ancient streets of that section of the city, where one fourth of the population was wiped out by an earthquake in 1755. We were very impressed with the Sintra, the summer palace of royalty when Portugal was a world power.

As lovers of the seaside, we were attracted to the southern section of Portugal, the Algarve. It was beautiful, and we were there in the early summer. Not only was there coastline natural beauty, but the dozens of naked women on the beach rapidly accelerated the depletion of my film supply.

One of the "must see" attractions in the ancient city of Faro was a Catholic church where the inside stucco walls were imbedded with literally hundreds of human skulls. We learned that these were remains of Protestants who were killed during the years of the Inquisition. When we got back home, I confronted a very Papist friend about the horrible treatment of my enlightened forebears by the Roman Catholic Church. Falling back on our humorous bantering over religious differences in the past, she retorted, "Well, they deserved it!"

After several refreshing days exploring the Algarve, we boarded a bus heading back to Lisbon, where we would catch our flight back home.

The bus was practically empty, so Sandy and I took seats by the window several rows apart. Ahead of me sat an older man who was totally absorbed in the paperback he was reading. With the hum of the motor and the comfort of the very modern vehicle, not much time passed before I began to drift off. For years I have had a habit of letting out a very audible snort and jarring myself awake from what rapidly becomes a deep sleep. My eyes closed and my head eased back on the headrest and just as I was about to enter dreamland, I gave out this very loud snort, which must have sounded something like a wild boar. The old guy sitting in the seat so engrossed in his reading, jerked upright and threw his book into the air. While it must have been quite an unexpected shock to him, it sent me into fits of stifled laughter. In another quarter of an hour however, I found myself dozing off and praying that I once again not sound like something stomping around in the jungle.

CHAPTER THIRTEEN—TOSSING IN THE SPONGE

The Retirement Decision

In 1995, I retired from full-time teaching at Hudson Valley College. It was a terrific career, but after 35 years of full-time classroom teaching and student advisement, it was time for a new and different change of pace.

Teaching computer software packages had a lingering benefit, however. The college always seemed to need adjunct faculty in that area, and I hadn't planned on leaving the vicinity. For eight years, I would sign on as a late-afternoon adjunct, teaching a three-hour class one day a week for the fifteen-week semester. It kept my mind alert, and it provided some extra cash. Besides, I had always loved to teach.

Teaching computer classes, however, was a constant challenge. Both the hardware and the software were continuously evolving. Things were never the same from one semester to the next. It wasn't like teaching Ancient Greek History or Calculus. I had to be constantly on the alert for innovations.

Harvard on the Hudson

There finally came a time to call it quits. When one senses that he is one step behind the students, one should step aside. Two occurrences prompted my decision to finally give up on teaching computer software classes. The first was the changing attitude of some of the students. In a word, the adjective "flaky" seemed to be more and more the norm. Many students would drift in and out of class with reckless abandon. I suspect that most students joining the class had already experienced a lot of computer preparation and thus, particularly at the beginning of the class, it all seemed so repetitious. They would tend to stop attending class, and when they eventually decided to return, it was too late. New and unfamiliar material had been introduced, and several quizzes had been administered.

One young man in particular contributed to what may be called "the final straw" in my decision to give up part-time teaching. Of the fifteen-week semester, he attended the first two sessions and then reappeared at the eleventh session. I had long ago written him off as a drop out. After class, he casually meandered to my desk and asked, "How can I get an 'A' in this class and what do I have to do to make up the work I've missed?"

"You sure have a lot of moxie," I thought to myself. "You have taken upon yourself to miss at least two thirds of the classes, assignments, and quizzes and you expect me to give you a helping hand. That's not going to happen."

"The answer to the first part of your question is that there is no way you will get anything close to an 'A,'" I told him, "because you simply haven't pulled your share of the load. As to the second part of the question, there's no way to make up the work, since you simply decided not to participate in the class when you had the opportunity."

I'd been seeing more and more of this type of flakiness as the years passed and assumed things would only be getting worse. Future contact with teaching colleagues assured me that my perception was accurate.

The second factor was pure and simple obsolescence — mine. At the outset of my final semester in teaching, a student came to me after class and most politely asked me why we were still using floppy disks instead of a flash drive to store data. To be honest, I had never even seen a flash drive, also known as a thumb drive.

"They are so far ahead of me that it's becoming an embarrassment," I thought to myself. Toward the middle of that winter semester of 2004, I decided to toss in the sponge and informed my chairperson of the decision. It was time to go.

Post Retirement Winters

In the latter years of our married life, Sandy became more and more independent. As mentioned earlier in the book, she had bought her own new car without telling me about it beforehand. A few years later, she put a "FOR SALE" sign on the house, and we moved to a town house to discourage our grown children from moving back home. Again, she did this without consulting me. It didn't bother me that much, however, because she had a knack for making the right decisions over the years, and I had come to respect her judgment.

Not long after I retired from full-time teaching, Sandy decided to get away from winter in the northeast by renting a unit in a gated trailer park on the lower East Coast of Florida. I had no desire to join her. To me, Florida is just too flat, and it has too many old people. Besides, I was still very active in church, and I enjoyed teaching part time as an adjunct at the college.

With this in mind, I stood my ground and gave her my decision. "I won't be going to Florida with you!" I firmly stated. Her response: "Who asked you to?" We worked out a compromise whereby I would fly down and join her in February for a week or two. This proved to be a very satisfactory arrangement.

Staying there for a brief period enabled me to take a lot of walks and to enjoy the community swimming pool in warm weather. Seeing the rich vegetation, eating out, and going to the beach were added benefits, too.

The golden oldies were certainly an interesting lot. One time I was lolling at poolside in the sunshine when this nearby octogenarian directed her husband, "Arthur, walk over there and take a look at the water temperature gauge. I can't see it from here. I swear the pool is a lot cooler than it was yesterday." The old guy obediently got up from his reclining chair and tottered over to the far end of the pool. When he returned, he informed his wife that the water temperature was 83 degrees, to which she responded, "See, I told you the water is colder today; yesterday it was 84." Ah, the glories of old age!

The Saddest Day

In the fourth winter of going south, Sandy was overcome with stomach cramps a few weeks before she was scheduled to drive back home. She went to a local hospital, and after an examination, she was told that there was a gastric problem. Sandy, who had many years of experience in the medical field as a nursing home administrator and also as a home caregiver, knew her problem was more serious than a gastric one. She came home a few weeks early.

We immediately made an appointment at a respected Albany hospital. Things had gotten worse, and we had no idea of the cause. Even at her hospital exploratory interview, in spite of her discomfort, Sandy maintained her sense of humor. The interviewer asked her several questions in order to determine what could be causing the problem. I sat next to my wife as she went through the interviewing process. One question the woman asked was, "Could this discomfort be related in any way to alcohol use?" Without a pause, Sandy, who seldom imbibed, shot a glance at me and answered, "Not unless it's contagious!" The nurse had to stifle her laughter.

Ovarian cancer. Stage three. That was the eventual diagnosis.

The oncologist was renowned, but he could only do so much. Over the months, he experimented with a variety of chemo treatments, but there never was any improvement. Nausea and diarrhea plagued this wonderful person unmercifully. Her health declined steadily until she had to make a decision regarding continuation of treatment. Throughout the ordeal, our large family was constantly involved, providing whatever help they could contribute—laundry, meals, cleaning, and just being there for moral support.

A good friend, now a Florida resident, spent several days in the area. At the latter stage of her illness, Sandy was so weak that she couldn't participate in a conversation, so the good friend and I sat on opposite sides of the bed and chatted with each other about happier times. Sandy could only smile and nod occasionally.

As a group, the family had a final interview with the oncologist in his office. We had beforehand assigned who would ask what question just to eliminate confusion. My daughter-in-law asked her assigned question, "Doctor, if this were your own mother, what advice would you give her?" In a flash came the answer from this seasoned professional, "My mother hasn't taken a word of my advice in her life, and I'm sure she wouldn't take any now or in the future." That provided the lighter moment of the session.

The final outcome became more and more obvious. Sandy was delivered the news in a most shocking manner, however. While my son and I were visiting her during one of her hospital stays, a young doctor stopped in. "Your doctor is on vacation, and I am taking his place for a while," he said. "I want you to know that we will be doing our best to make you comfortable from here on out!" That was it—probably the worst example of bedside manner I've ever experienced. Instead of a private meeting with perhaps a few family members in attendance and some reassuring lead-in, this guy just dropped the unmistakable bomb that there was no more that could be done. Sandy and I and our son were shocked into silence.

Weeks earlier, however, my wife had surmised that further efforts were futile. She had had so much experience with dying patients that she knew the end was near.

At this point, she asked us to contact Hospice. That organization is, in a word, wonderful. There was continuous psychological and medical help provided at home by professionals. They were caring and capable and so very thoughtful in those final weeks. We had been told to expect to have Sandy with us at home for about three more months.

Harvard on the Hudson

Her decline was accelerating, and after only three weeks, the Hospice nurse took me aside and said, "It is time for you to gather all of your family together. She can't last more than a day or two more, and I think it may be as early as late tonight!"

That final day was the most memorable one of my life. After several months of misery, Sandy and those of us closest to her had reconciled ourselves to the fact that it was time for the book to close.

I remember phoning my daughter who lived near Philadelphia, saying, "Heather, you have to come home now. It's time." I clearly recall her saying, "But Dad, they said she had three months. It can't be so soon."

The immediate family gathered at our townhouse by two in the afternoon. There was no end of activity. Cold-water packs were applied continuously. Morphine was administered when she needed it, as suggested by Hospice. In a daze, we talked and ate snacks sent in by friends. I never felt so blessed in my entire life because my entire family comforted me with love and caring. We shared so many fond reminiscences as the hours ticked by. Sandy was in the upstairs bedroom, and we took turns sitting at her bedside. Her last sign of activity came at about eight p.m. She had been breathing sporadically for hours when she briefly opened her eyes and smiled. She weakly waved her fingers in a farewell gesture and then closed her eyes. Just before midnight she passed on. How I loved that woman, and how proud I was of my family on that final day.

The younger ones had a very hard time letting go, and I could see no sense in hastening the process. I asked the funeral director to stand by until all of us had said our farewells. It was three hours before my youngest could bring herself to leave the bedside.

At the memorial service, the church was packed. It was upbeat service, with so many sharing cheerful remembrances.

Sandy loved the ocean, particularly the craggy coast at Rockport on Cape Ann, Massachusetts. Her wish was to have her ashes spread in the sea. She sure got her wish. I scattered some of them into the sea at Rockport. But I did more than that: ashes have also been cast in the sea at Florida, California, Hawaii, Tahiti, Australia, and Thailand. I did, however, save a small quantity to rest with me in the family cemetery overlooking the homestead.

CHAPTER FOURTEEN—LIFE AFTER LOSS

After the loss of an irreplaceable life-long companion, there is often a lengthy period of grieving and despondency. For me, that dreaded period was relatively brief. For one thing, after several months of Sandy's suffering with the certainty of passing, the loss for me was, in large measure, a blessing. In addition, I had the comfort of a large, close-knit family and friends who consistently gave me their love and attention. After a few months, I was able to shed much of the despair and get on with my life.

Selling the Car

My wife had bought a used Toyota a year or so before she passed on. At that time, I had a sturdy pickup truck, and I also drove the Model A Ford in the warmer weather. It just didn't seem sensible to me to own and operate three vehicles, so I decided to advertise her car in the local newspaper. I spent hours preparing the ad to ensure that I was offering a most attractive used car.

Previous to advertising it, I spent $150 having the car detailed. The ad cost an additional $50.

The following morning, I anxiously scanned the advertising section to make sure there were no errors in the wording of the ad. There were none.

In fact, the ad was so attractive that I thought to myself, "Why would anyone in their right mind want to sell a great car like that?"

So I canceled the ad at a net cost of $200! The car served me faithfully for several more years.

Fond Memories

As time passes and the memories recur, I think of so many clever things Sandy said over the years.

One such memory involves a conversation she and I and my nephew Reg from northern New York State had regarding my retirement plans.

"You say you are definitely retiring. What do you plan to do with yourself once you are no longer teaching?" Reg asked me.

"I'm really looking forward to spending time doing those things I most enjoy. I love travel, swimming, spending time with my family, and working with my hands," I replied.

To involve Sandy in the conversation, Reg asked her, "Just what does he like to do with his hands?"

"Oh, I don't know," she demurely replied, "Most of the time on those private occasions my eyes are closed."

Harvard on the Hudson

<u>Gambling Advice</u>

Sandy and I enjoyed playing the slot machines. She often came out ahead of the game and I invariably lost. In fact, I lost just about everywhere we played: Atlantic City, Foxwoods, Las Vegas, and even in Uruguay (Puente del Este), Portugal, and Austria.

When we were in Salzburg, Austria, Sandy grew tired of my complaints about losing roughly $200.

"You just don't know how to play the slots," she admonished. "You spend a little time at a lot of different machines. You have no patience. I stay with one machine all the time, and that's why I win."

It sounded like good advice to me. After all, my approach simply wasn't working.

The next night, we returned to the same casino, and I stuck with her advice like glue. And I lost another $200!

I groused, "I did exactly what you told me to do. I stayed on one machine all night, and I lost another $200."

"And I suppose you're going to blame me for that!" she snapped back at me.

Not only couldn't I win at the slots, I couldn't win with her either!

W. L. Staats

Thailand and Cambodia

Although Sandy had passed away, I still had the yearning to travel. So I took a real chance on the Internet and booked a three-week trip to Thailand and Cambodia. Finding that the flight over was a non-stop, 20-hour ordeal, I was concerned about the discomfort factor. I talked with a good friend of my daughter's who was a worldwide traveler due to his work with an international bank.

"Is it possible to get some rest?" I asked. "I never sleep well in a sitting position and besides the damned seats are uncomfortably narrow and confining,"

"You know what works for me?" he replied. "I just order some wine and take one Ambien tablet. It does the trick."

That sounded like good advice, but just to be safe I checked in with my Czech doctor. "You haff had two bypass operations and several stents inserted," she cautioned me. "If you take vine and an Ambien, you vill not vake up when you get to Thailand!" So I suffered the discomfort.

It occurred to me that I might have done something extremely naive by booking the trip on the internet through a tourist agency located in Bangkok. For all I knew, the office could have been located upstairs over a vacant parking lot. What a pleasant surprise greeted me at the airport. There awaited a new Toyota with a Thai driver and an interpreter. I was treated like royalty. For five days, I traveled about the hinterlands of the Asian capital city, but I must admit becoming worn out from climbing the steps of an endless succession of temples. My Thai hosts went out of their way to make my visit a wonderful experience. I stayed in well-appointed hotels and made sure to avoid eating food from street vendors. No sense taking a chance with digestive problems so far from home.

When I left Bangkok, I flew south to the paradise resort of Puchet famous for its oceanside natural beauty. Exotic beaches and a boat cruise to remote rock formations were unforgettable.

When registering at the hotel, the clerk was most efficient. One inquiry, however, just about floored me. "Will you be having a woman in your room?" she asked. "If so," she continued, "there will be an additional charge of $50 a day."

I supposed I should have been complimented by the suggestion that, at my age, I was still a tiger at heart. However, I answered, "Please take a good look at me. I'm 75 years old, bald, fat and wrinkled, and my plumbing is completely shot. Do you really think I'll be bringing a woman up to my room?"

She smiled broadly, and I know she had fun sharing the conversation with her hotel colleagues because they, too, smiled when greeting me.

After five days in Thailand, I took a small plane to Siem Reap, Cambodia, with the express purpose of seeing Angkor Wat, the world's largest temple complex. It was a good drive from the hotel, but my Cambodian team of driver and interpreter didn't seem to mind conveying me to the site several times. It was mesmerizing to marvel at the centuries-old structure with its five spires. Apparently, Angkor Wat, which was built at the direction of a Khmer king in the early 12th century, was subsequently occupied by Buddhists and then later abandoned. It became overgrown with vines and trees, and it has taken decades to bring it to its current majestic form.

I was really intrigued by some of the delicacies peddled by street vendors: fried beetles and hairy spiders and ants had some allure, but common sense prevailed over the desire to try out these rare delicacies.

Cambodia has a noticeably lower standard of living than Thailand. Many villages were located on polluted waterways. Poverty was rampant. Still, the people were smiling and friendly.

I took a 10-hour motorized boat ride south from Siem Reap to the capital of Cambodia, Phnom Penh. That city has seen truly hard times. Some two million people were brutally murdered by the Khmer Rouge under Pol Pot. He had a vendetta against intellectuals, fearing that they would stir up civil unrest. He killed thousands simply because they wore glasses—an indicator that they could read!

The city has a number of museums and burial sites that depict the shocking holocaust of the "killing fields." It was most unsettling, and it produced indelible memories of horror.

Travel with a Friend

Renee Calder has been a friend for more than 60 years. She was widowed when her husband, my best buddy in high school days, died from complications associated with Alzheimer's. She'd had twelve years of care giving. When I lost my wife to cancer, my friendship with Renee continued, mainly because of her vibrancy.

I worked up the courage to ask her to travel with me, recalling clearly her puritan convictions. Our first trip was an Island-hopping adventure in Hawaii. What a terrific experience!

Since Renee had flown in from Florida and I from New York State, we decided to catch up with each other in Honolulu on Oahu. It was such a treat to meet a close friend with whom to share the sites. When traveling, we always specified separate beds. Not only did it stifle urges, but snoring had become a mutual problem that we hadn't planned on. She would accuse me of making endless groaning sounds, and I had trouble deciphering the occasional murmurs she muttered.

In what seemed like the middle of our first night in Honolulu together, I heard the shower running. I glanced at my watch and it read 4 a.m. Renee was talking a shower at that unearthly hour! When she completed her shower and had put on her robe, she returned to the bedroom. "Do you always take a shower at four in the morning?" I inquired.

Renee lost it. "Four o'clock!! I can't believe it. I looked at my watch and it said it was nine." And then it struck her. She had forgotten to set the time on her watch to account for the change in time zones! I never saw anyone leap back into bed and go back to sleep in such a hurry!

Oahu is lovely, but really too "touristy." We enjoyed Waikiki Beach adjacent to our hotel, and we toured the Navy base at Pearl Harbor.

On the big Island of Hawaii, we rented a car and drove to a Kona coffee plantation. We also visited luxurious tropical forest parks and often marveled at the cascading waterfalls and the gorgeous array of orchids.

On Maui, we enjoyed an evening cocktail party aboard a catamaran. We also pigged out at a sumptuous luau.

Harvard on the Hudson

On the quiet but beautiful island of Kauai, we thrilled at driving to the crest of Waimea Canyon. Our hotel was located on a secluded beach. The relaxed pace was most inviting after several days of seeing the other islands.

With that successful adventure behind us, two years or so later, Renee and I scheduled a trip to New Zealand and Australia. It would be another opportunity for me to renew friendships with Aussie colleagues.

But before New Zealand—Tahiti. After all, it was on the way! This time around, I was bound and determined to spend a few days at Bora Bora. This island paradise had always captured my imagination. Unfortunately, compared with another Tahitian island, Moorea, which Sandy and I had previously visited, Bora Bora was a disappointment. Some of the problem may have stemmed from my decision to use the Club Med facilities.

Bora Bora itself was enchanting. The facility, however, left something to be desired. The Club Med plan included meals and booze as well as accommodations. Sounds great, right? Not really. For instance, the entertainment was provided by employees of Club Med. At Moorea, native Tahitians provided the music, which was so much more authentic than that of Club Med. The free drinks were so weak that Renee and I would order a gin and tonic and then supplement it with a shot of pure gin.

We were ensconced in a thatched roof hut that was a lengthy walk from the main lodge. And, oh boy, were we surprised to see a king-sized bed instead of the double beds we preferred for modesty, privacy, and temptation's sake. We looked at each other with that "What do we do now?" look. The solution: we bundled, and it worked out fine. There were no sexual overtures, and somehow we managed to get through the snoring situation. At least we took advantage of all the facility had to offer. The meals were plentiful and exotic. We did some snorkel swimming at a nearby reef. Beach walking and enjoying a glass-bottom boat ride were fun.

After Bora Bora, our plane landed in Queenstown, New Zealand, a very beautiful resort town on the South Island. There we found that in terms of interests we sometimes disagreed. Renee was very thrifty; I'm extravagant. She loves to shop— to me it's an anathema. I was intrigued by our visit to the glowworm caves; she felt claustrophobic and concerned about the unsteady wooden walkways throughout the cave. I worried about her driving, particularly on the left side of the road as is customary in New Zealand. I didn't mind getting too close to the fence posts, until I realized that they were on my side of the car! Many months later, I found out that Renee was terrified of my driving as well. Too much casual sightseeing while behind the wheel was the main complaint!

In spite of our differences, we loved New Zealand with its pastoral scenery and the charm of garden-rich Christchurch.

Harvard on the Hudson

Returning to Australia was like coming home. I knew so many teaching colleagues, and Renee was such an asset, with her deep interest in flowers and people. At one dinner, a randy associate of mine asked Renee if she and I were bed partners. That somewhat shattered her reserve. We had a wonderful time staying with Allen and Pam Holmes, enjoying their inviting Melbourne residence and also their beach house. We drove the Great Ocean Road.

After leaving Melbourne, we stopped for two days at Sydney, and thoroughly enjoyed touring the beautiful harbor city. We got used to the subway and took a harbor cruise, which gave us the chance to see the opera house, the harbor bridge, and the Toronga Park Zoo. Overall, we had a magnificent vacation together.

CHAPTER FIFTEEN—THE WRAP UP

Time has marched on and on and on for the author. Looking back, there is a feeling of deep gratitude for this most enjoyable lifetime adventure. I have been blessed in so many ways.

The first fortunate turn of events had nothing to do with choices. I was born into a terrific family. We had very little in terms of financial resources, but we were much more compensated for that by love and good fortune. Although we lost my father at a very early age at the beginning of the Great Depression, relatives and friends combined efforts to enable my mother and her seven young offspring to survive and even thrive.

Not only was there the blessing of a fine family, but also the awesome experience of being brought up in a seventeenth century homestead on the east bank of the Hudson River — which has been owned and occupied by our family for twelve generations. Country living, with its opportunities for activity and the responsibility of maintenance work, has also provided invaluable memories.

Harvard on the Hudson

My first important decision was to enter the teaching profession — I loved all 47 years of it. Attending an inexpensive teacher's college and subsequently pursuing secondary school and later college teaching were ideal for this writer. The community college experience was particularly rewarding to the extent that even a decade after retiring, close friendships have been maintained with administrators, staff, faculty and students.

The second wise decision was to join the Navy for a two-year stint. It took me away from home and it provided time to sort out lifetime goals. It also supplied a few more lasting friends.

The third and most important decision was in choosing a life partner. Sandy was the ideal wife — intelligent, hard-working, physically attractive, humorous — destined to be a fine friend, wife, mother, grandmother, caregiver and all around great companion.

Becoming involved in an urban inner-city church was another wise decision. Serving as treasurer and being involved in the choir for forty years have provided even more friendships as well as a wealth of practical accounting (we never failed an audit) and great music experience.

Another rewarding decision was to spend a year teaching at and Australian college. Why that course of action? For me, life was becoming a routine in the 1960's and there was that latent element of wanderlust. And, too, Australia had a compatible climate and there would be no language barrier. I never imagined that this experience would produce so many treasured memories and that there would be so many lasting friendships with my Aussie teaching colleagues.

The recent years have become quieter. Physical infirmities have set in which have severely restricted activity, but there have been compensations. Appreciation for reading and savoring family and friendships are now more important than ever. And too, one can never spend enough time just sitting on the veranda and enjoying the view of the Hudson.

Your Reaction to the Book is Important

After reading "Harvard on the Hudson" it would be very much appreciated if you would communicate to the author, W. L. Staats, which three of the anecdotes in the book you consider to be the most enjoyable. ***Your name will remain anonymous***. This information could provide useful background for future reference in terms of content for speaking engagements and other promotional activities.

The author can be reached by E-mail at hoogebergh@aol.com or by telephone at 518-477-5765